STUDY GUIDE: TOOLS FOR SUCCESS

PRINCIPLES OF
MACROECONOMICS

FRED GOTTHEIL

PREPARED BY
DAVID WISHART
WITTENBERG UNIVERSITY

SOUTH-WESTERN College Publishing
An International Thomson Publishing Company

Acquisitions Editor: Jack C. Calhoun
Publisher/Team Director: Valerie A. Ashton
Developmental Editor: Dennis Hanseman
Production Editor: Rebecca Roby
Cover Design: Design Crew
Cover Illustration: © Michael David Brown
Team Assistants: Ronda Faulkner, B.J. Barker, Cory Broadfoot

Copyright © 1996
by South-Western College Publishing
Cincinnati, Ohio

ALL RIGHTS RESERVED
The text of this publication, or any part thereof, may not be reproduced or transmitted in any form or by any means, electronic or mechanical, including photocopying, recording, storage in an information retrieval system, or otherwise, without prior written permission from the publisher.

ISBN: 0-538-87156-3
1 2 3 4 5 6 7 PN 2 1 0 9 8 7 6
Printed in the United States of America

I(T)P

International Thomson Publishing
South-Western College Publishing is an ITP Company. The ITP trademark is used under license.

TABLE OF CONTENTS

Preface   iv

Part I   The Basics of Economic Analysis

1. Introduction   1
2. Production Possibilities and Opportunity Costs   11
3. Demand and Supply   22

Part II   Employment, Inflation, and Fiscal Policy

4. Aggregate Demand and Aggregate Supply   34
5. Gross Domestic Product Accounting   46
6. Building the Keynesian Model: Consumption and Investment   56
7. Equilibrium National Income in the Keynesian Model   66
8. Fiscal Policy: Coping with Inflation and Unemployment   76
9. Economic Growth, Business Cycles, and Countercyclical Fiscal Policy   86

Part III   Money, Banking, and Monetary Policy

10. Money   95
11. Money Creation and the Banking System   104
12. The Federal Reserve System and Monetary Policy   112

Part IV   Government and the Economy

13. Can Government Really Stabilize the Economy?   121
14. Government Spending   131
15. Financing Government: Taxes and Debt   139

Part V   The World Economy

16. International Trade   149
17. Exchange Rates, Balance of Payments, and International Debt   160
18. Economic Problems of Less-Developed Countries   171
19. Theories of Comparative Economic Systems   180

PREFACE

My first contact with Fred Gottheil came some 25 years ago when my Dad enlisted my aid typing a long, long book review as part of Professor Gottheil's graduate level History of Economic Thought course that he was taking at the University of Illinois. Typing was one of the most useful things I learned in junior high school and my Dad, no slouch as an economist, knew how to exploit cheap labor effectively. I think I made 50 cents per page. It was either that or mow the yard. Never in my widest 13-year-old imagination would I have dreamed that I'd go on to major in economics after having taken Fred's Principles of Economics course at Illinois (largely to defend myself in arguments with my Dad), then become good friends with Fred, write my Ph.D. thesis under his supervision, and be involved in a major textbook/study guide project with him spanning some 14 years. I can say without hesitation that working with Fred has been one of the joys of my life. I owe him an enormous debt of gratitude for teaching me about economics and much more. That Fred is a wonderful soul comes through in his text.

Writing this study guide has proven to be fun and rewarding. I haven't done it alone. Hundreds of my students at Wittenberg University have been subjected to dozens of true-false, multiple choice, and discussion questions, many of which appear in this book. My students have been quick to point out flaws in my questions and their editing suggestions have greatly improved the final product. They have instructed me on how to be a better teacher. I am especially thankful to the following students who went so far as to write some multiple choice questions for possible use in the book. They are Deborah Goldstein, Ed Hasecke, Chris Murray, Kristen Neubauer, Ryan Terry, Steve Valenti, and Bethany Young. My research assistant, Mojca Fink, deserves great credit for reading the whole manuscript and pointing out numerous mistakes to be corrected. She has a great eye for detail—not one of my strengths as Professor Gottheil will tell you. Even so, I'm certain there are mistakes yet to be corrected. They are my responsibility and I'm counting on students to alert me to them so that the product can be improved further. Please contact me by e-mail with comments on the book at WISHRT@WITTENBERG.EDU. Thanks go also to my editors at South-Western College Publishing, Jack Calhoun, Dennis Hanseman, and Rebecca Roby. They've been enormously positive and helpful in this endeavor.

Finally, I give special thanks to my wife Jo Wilson who has been so patient and supportive over many months of writing and to my children Tony and Jacob who have put up with a distracted parent for too long. My happiness stems directly from their love and affection.

CHAPTER 1

INTRODUCTION

Chapter Summary

If everyone had everything they ever wanted and were assured that they would have everything they ever want in the forever future, there would be no economics. Can you even imagine it? Alas, it's about as farfetched a fiction as we can dream! The real world is nothing like it. Economics exists because *we live in a world of scarcity*. It means that the quantity of resources available to us—which we use to make goods and services—is limited by the finiteness of our world, but our demands for these goods and services are virtually unlimited. Even though we may discover new resources, we are forever discovering, at the same time, new demands as well. That creates a problem. Because our demands always outstrip our supply of resources to satisfy them, we find ourselves always having to make choices—which goods to produce and which not. *Scarcity creates our need to choose.*

Let's look at the idea of limited resources. We have so many resources—discovered and undiscovered—and that's it. Economists differentiate between renewable and nonrenewable resources. Renewable resources regenerate over time. A forest, if harvested for lumber at the same rate that new trees grow, can be maintained forever. But other resources, such as copper and zinc, are nonrenewable. When we use them, we deplete them.

Our economic world is a complicated one. Millions of people work producing many millions of goods. Which goods are produced, how they are produced and who gets them is what economics is about. To study these questions, economists look not only at the real world—which is sometimes too complex to appreciate—but at a simple representation of that real world. The key word here is *simple*. This representation is called an economic model. The idea is this: If we can understand how the simple model of an economy works, it may give us clues about how the more complicated real-world economy works. The circular flow of money, goods and services, described in the text, is an example of an economic model. It is a model of households and firms buying and selling resources, goods and services from each other. The beauty of this model is that it shows how people earn income and why firms produce the goods and services they do. Economic models rely heavily on the assumption of *ceteris paribus,* which means that the functional relationships in the model assume everything else is held constant.

The study of economics is divided into two fields—microeconomics and macroeconomics. Microeconomists focus on *individual units* such as consumers, firms, industries, and markets. The analysis looks at their behavior with respect to price formation. Macroeconomists focus on *aggregates,* that is, the economy as a whole. The questions discussed include: Why do nations grow? Why are there business cycles? What causes national unemployment and inflation?

Economists also differentiate between positive economics—an analysis of what is—and normative economics—an analysis of what ought to be. Positive economic analysis is free from value judgments while normative economic analysis expresses value judgments. Most economists work in positive economics. There is nothing wrong with normative economics, but we must be careful to identify it as value judgment.

As simplifications of reality, economic models are frequently presented as graphs and/or equations. The graphs and equations that economists use are pictorial or mathematical representations of concepts that could be expressed in words. However, if these concepts were described in words they would be harder to understand. The purpose of graphs and equations is to allow us to see relationships more clearly. Some of the following exercises will test your ability to work with graphs and equations.

THE BASICS — CHAPTER 1 INTRODUCTION

Key Terms — Test your comprehension by defining and explaining the significance of these terms. Terms from the appendix to this chapter are included in this list.

natural resources	macroeconomics
limitless or insatiable wants	positive economics
scarcity	normative economics
economics	econometrics
consumer sovereignty	point of reference
social sciences	independent variable
abstraction	dependent variable
economic model	slope of a curve
ceteris paribus	negatively sloped curve
circular flow model	positively sloped curve
household	tangent
firm	slope of a tangent
microeconomics	

True-False Questions — If a statement is false, explain why.

1. Economists regard natural resources as gifts of nature. (T/F)

2. In the absence of advertising, people's wants would not be insatiable. (T/F)

3. It follows that if resources are limited and people's wants are insatiable, then scarcity exists. (T/F)

4. Economics is the study of how people make money in the stock market. (T/F)

5. Economists use complex graphs and models to explain how simple real-world economies work. (T/F)

6. An economic model is an exact representation of an economy. (T/F)

7. The circular flow model would better represent the real world if flows of money, resources, goods and services to and from government were included. (T/F)

8. The *ceteris paribus* assumption is often used to simplify economic analysis. (T/F)

9. Economics is a branch of the social sciences because it focuses on individual and social behavior. (T/F)

10. Microeconomics is more useful than macroeconomics because it gives a more detailed picture of the economy. (T/F)

11. Macroeconomic analysis focuses on economic activity at an aggregate rather than at an individual level. (T/F)

12. Positive economics is involved in policy formation, stating positively what ought to be. (T/F)

13. Normative economics involves value judgments. (T/F)

14. An economist hired to plan economic policies for a presidential candidate would never engage in positive economic analysis. (T/F)

15. Because social scientists work with models that are precise representations of the world's social systems, it is possible for them to draw precise conclusions about the nature of social problems. (T/F)

Multiple Choice Questions

1. The difference between a renewable resource and a nonrenewable resource is that
   a. a renewable resource can never be depleted while a nonrenewable resource is depleted as it is used.
   b. a nonrenewable resource can never be depleted while a renewable resource is depleted as it is used.
   c. the stock of a renewable resource can be maintained forever.
   d. conservation efforts cannot save renewable resources.
   e. renewable resources are liquids, nonrenewable resources are solids.

2. Economics is a social science that explores the problem of
   a. how society transforms scarce resources into goods and services.
   b. using graphs to describe complex relationships.
   c. recycling scarce resources to make them more useful to society.
   d. what ought to be done to make the world a better place.
   e. economics is *not* a social science.

3. All of the following characterize a world without scarcity except
   a. there would be even more crime and violence because people would fight over all the goods.
   b. there would be no need for economists.
   c. there would be no reason to save.
   d. there would be no reason to economize on scarce resources.
   e. new and unlimited demands would continue to grow.

4. Positive economics deals with _____ while normative economics considers _____.
   a. what ought to be; what is
   b. what is; what ought to be
   c. good policies; policies for normal times
   d. improvements in living standards; how to keep the economy steady over time
   e. a positive approach to economic problems; normal approach to problems

5. Microeconomics is the branch of economics that analyzes _____ while macroeconomics is the branch of economics that analyzes _____.
   a. the behavior of individual economic units; how national economies work
   b. how national economies work; the behavior of individual economic units
   c. positive questions; normative questions
   d. historical issues on a micro scale; contemporary issues on a large scale
   e. economic details, broader aspects of economic issues

6. In the circular flow model, households furnish labor, capital, land, and entrepreneurship to businesses for which they are paid _____, _____, _____, and _____, respectively.
   a. profit, interest, rent, wages
   b. wages, interest, rent, profit
   c. wages, interest, profit, rent
   d. wages, profits, interest, rent
   e. wages, rent, interest, profit

7. In a graph, the vertical axis represents the _____ and the horizontal axis represents the _____.
   a. quantity of a good; price of a good
   b. quantity of a good; cost of a good
   c. independent variable; dependent variable
   d. dependent variable; independent variable
   e. x variable; y variable

8. The term slope refers to
   a. change in the dependent variable divided by change in the independent variable.
   b. change in the independent variable divided by change in the dependent variable.
   c. graphs that are straight lines only.
   d. graphs that are curves only.
   e. the value of the dependent variable divided by the value of the independent variable.

9. This curve depicts
   a. a slope that is positive at first but decreases as x increases and eventually becomes negative.
   b. a slope that is always positive but decreases, then increases as x increases.
   c. a slope that is negative at first but becomes less negative as x increases and eventually becomes positive.
   d. the slope cannot be measured precisely since it isn't constant.
   e. the slope is always negative.

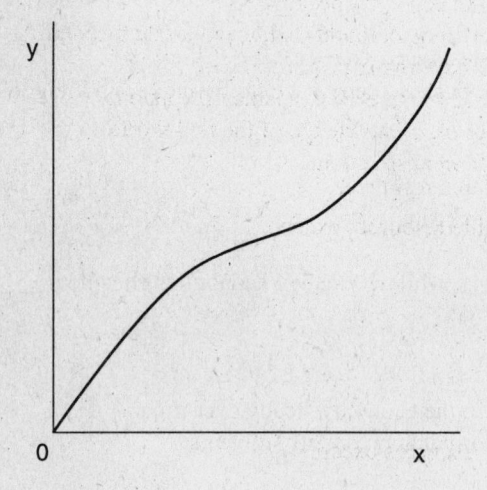

10. Models that economists use are
    a. perfect representations of the real world.
    b. typically useless oversimplifications of the real world.
    c. useful to the extent that assumptions underlying them are realistic.
    d. useful only if people in government can use them to formulate economic policy.
    e. useful only when other social scientists can understand them.

CHAPTER 1 INTRODUCTION   THE BASICS   5

11. Money flows in resource markets represent payments to _____ whereas money flows in product markets represent payments to _____.
    a. business firms; factors of production
    b. natural resource owners; other factors of production
    c. the government; private businesses
    d. property owners; only the most productive individuals
    e. factors of production; firms producing goods and services

12. Scarcity is a term used by economists to describe the fact that
    a. people's wants are insatiable.
    b. natural resources are available to us in fixed amounts.
    c. there will always be poverty in the world.
    d. abundance and affluence are never permanent.
    e. people's wants are insatiable relative to the availability of resources.

13. Which of the following statements is not a normative statement?
    a. Low income individuals ought to be exempt from income taxes.
    b. Unemployment and inflation should be minimized.
    c. Economic growth is sluggish.
    d. The government should cut funding for the arts.
    e. The money supply should grow at a constant rate.

14. Which of the following statements is not a positive statement?
    a. Prices of essential goods and services should be set by the government.
    b. The economy is extremely complex.
    c. People's wants are insatiable.
    d. Payments for resources are made in factor markets.
    e. Unemployment last year was 7.3 percent of the labor force.

15. Economists use abstractions in their analysis of the economy because
    a. information is insufficient to allow for detailed consideration of any economic problem.
    b. abstractions are useful when economic model-building is inappropriate.
    c. they want to reduce the complexity of the world to more manageable dimensions.
    d. abstractions are necessary to overcome gaps in their knowledge of the real world.
    e. the real world they want to understand is itself an abstraction.

16. All of the following are examples of nonrenewable resources except
    a. forests.
    b. iron ore.
    c. coal.
    d. oil.
    e. natural gas.

17. All of the following are examples of renewable resources except
    a. water.
    b. fisheries.
    c. gold.
    d. labor.
    e. corn.

18. A resource that is especially scarce during one period in human history
    a. will always be scarce since it is essential.
    b. may become less scarce as technologies change.
    c. should always be conserved carefully for future generations.
    d. is usually put under government control as the economy develops.
    e. is often depleted completely by overuse.

19. All of the following are issues of central focus for economists except
    a. Who produces what?
    b. What do governments do?
    c. How are goods and services produced?
    d. Who consumes what?
    e. Who decides what is produced, how it is produced, and who consumes?

20. Economists use the *ceteris paribus* assumption in order to
    a. increase the sophistication of their models.
    b. make it possible to study the way many variables change at once.
    c. minimize the need for abstraction.
    d. focus on one-to-one, cause-and-effect relationships.
    e. pursue microeconomic analysis rather than macroeconomic analysis.

Problems

1. a. Compute the slope of the following line.

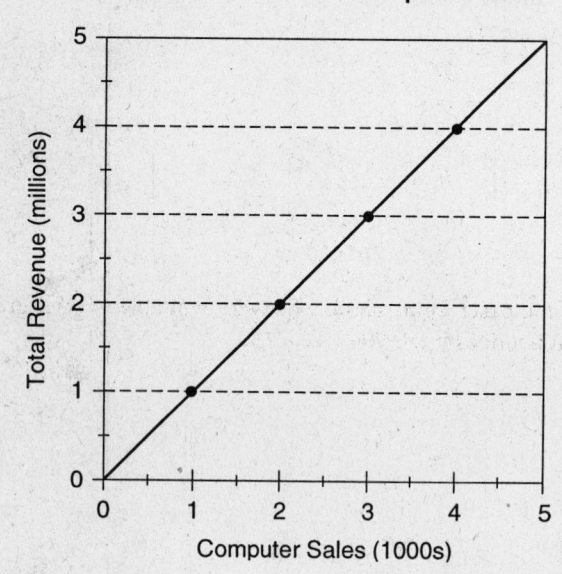

   Total Revenue from Computer Sales

   [Graph: vertical axis "Total Revenue (millions)" from 0 to 5; horizontal axis "Computer Sales (1000s)" from 0 to 5; line passes through points (1,1), (2,2), (3,3), (4,4).]

   b. The vertical axis is total revenue from sales of computers in millions of dollars and the horizontal axis represents the number of computers sold in thousands. How do you interpret the slope you computed?

CHAPTER 1   INTRODUCTION   THE BASICS   7

2. This diagram shows the situation a tomato seller faces in a crowded farmer's market. The farmer can sell as many tomatoes as he wants at $0.50 per bushel. Suppose this farmer sells 30 bushels of tomatoes. What is the total revenue the farmer receives? Show the total revenue on the graph.

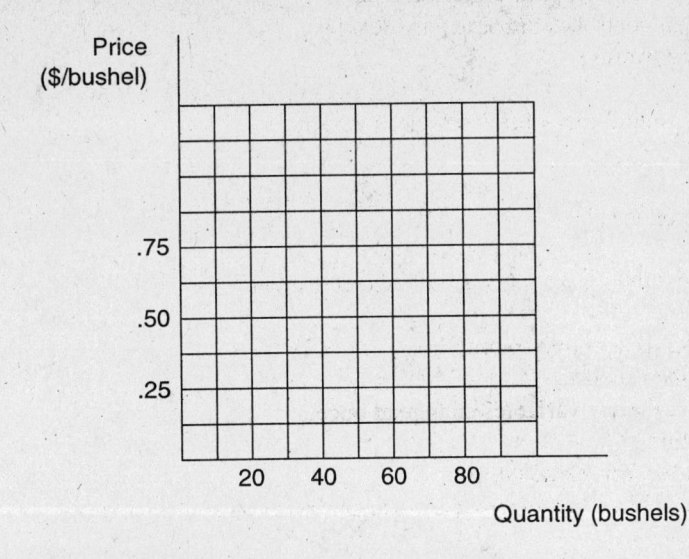

Price ($/bushel) vs Quantity (bushels)

Discussion Questions

1. Having read this introductory chapter, write down your impressions of what it is economists study and the methodology used by economists in their work.

2. Can you imagine scarcity becoming a thing of the past? Think about what was available to your grandparents compared to what you have at your disposal. What does it tell you?

3. Would a breakthrough in the production of energy, say the use of nuclear fusion, have an impact on scarcity in general? Explain.

4. Identify the slopes of the following curves as positive, negative, or both. If a curve shows both types of slopes, show where it is positive and where it is negative.

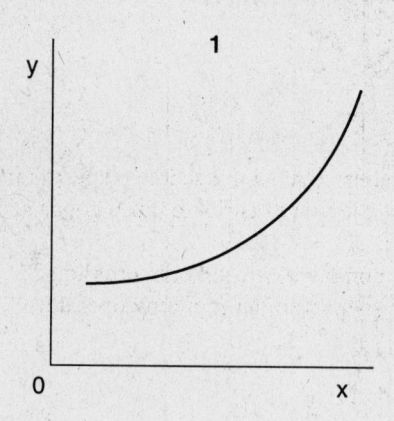

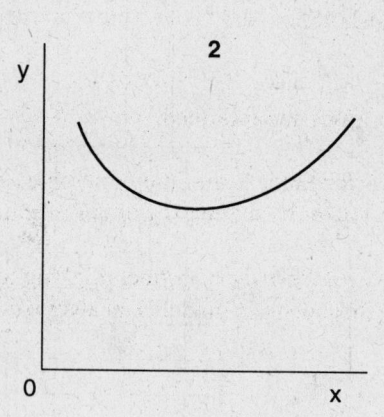

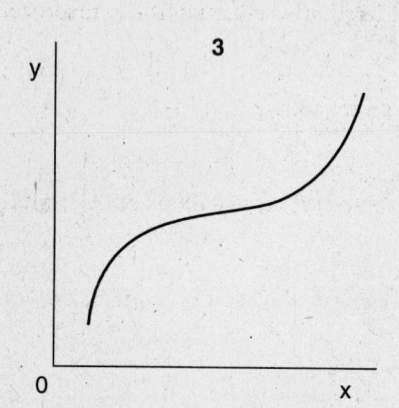

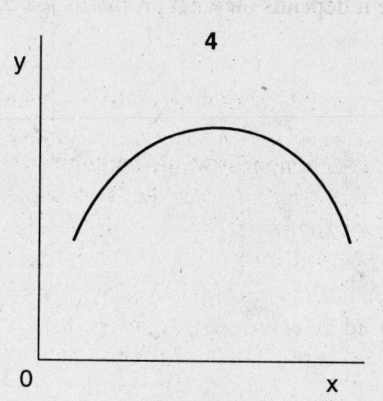

Answers to Questions

True-False Questions

1. True
2. False because wants are unlimited.
3. True
4. False because economics is the study of how we work together to transform scarce resources into goods and services to satisfy the most pressing of our infinite needs, and how we distribute those goods and services among ourselves.
5. False because economists use abstract thinking to simplify complicated economic problems.
6. False because an economic model is an abstraction of the way parts of an economy operate.
7. True
8. True
9. True
10. False because it depends on what problems are under consideration whether micro- or macroeconomics is more useful.
11. True
12. False because positive economics considers what exists in an economy.
13. True
14. False because the economist would certainly want correct facts.
15. False because the social sciences don't use models that are perfect representations of the world.

Multiple Choice Questions

1. c	6. b	11. e	16. a
2. a	7. d	12. e	17. c
3. a	8. a	13. c	18. b
4. b	9. b	14. a	19. b
5. a	10. c	15. c	20. d

Problems

1. a. Pick any two points on the line such as (x,y) = (0,0) and (x,y) = (5,10). The slope is the change in y divided by the change in x or, 10 – 0 / 5 – 0 = 2.

    b. If the slope is 2, then a 1000 computer increase in sales results in a $2 million increase in total revenue.

2. The diagram shows the revenue from tomato sales as the shaded gray region. Total revenue in this case is $0.50 × 30 bushels or $15.00.

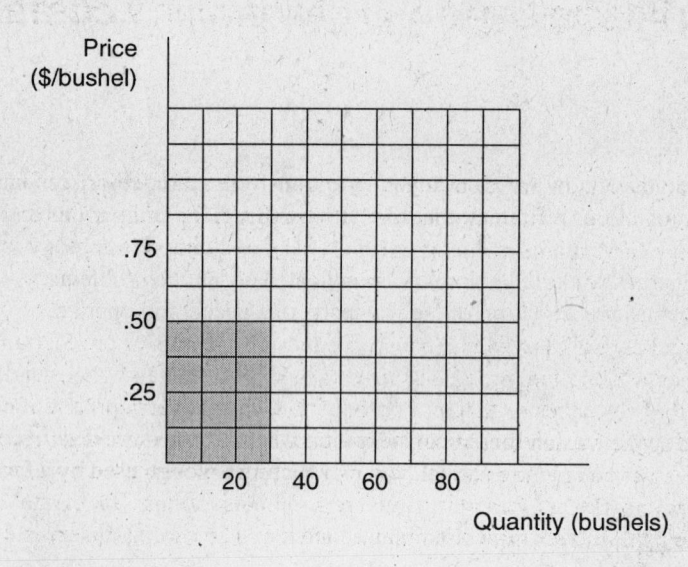

Discussion Questions

1. Economists study how societies cope with the problem of scarcity. For example, economists study the allocation of scarce resources for production of goods and services. Distribution of these goods and services is also a focus of analysis. Economists develop theoretical models to help them sort out the core issues in economic questions. It is possible to test these theoretical models against real-world data.

2. In recent history the advances of the industrial revolution have helped to diminish the severity of scarcity. Pick up a Sears catalog from the 1950s and look at the mix of goods that was available to American consumers then. Would you trade places with them today?

3. Yes indeed. A bountiful supply of cheap energy would greatly diminish the severity of energy scarcity. In general, technological advances reduce relative scarcity.

4. The first panel shows a positive slope, the second a negative then positive slope, the third is positive, and the fourth is positive then negative.

CHAPTER 2

PRODUCTION POSSIBILITIES AND OPPORTUNITY COSTS

Chapter Summary

Economists use language that often appears to be rather ordinary, such as money, cost, labor, and land, but the meanings they attach to these words are more often than not quite different from the ordinary meanings other people attach to them. This chapter introduces and explains some of the every-day-sounding terminology that makes up the economist's language.

If you know how to bake a cake, you know what economists mean by factors of production and goods and services. Factors of production or resources are the ingredients used to bake the cake, and goods and services refer to the cake itself. Economists identify four resources or factors of production. Two of these productive factors—labor and entrepreneurship—are described as the human factors and two—capital and land—are described as non-human. It's not quite as simple as it may appear. If you picture capital, you may picture a plough used by a farmer to till a field or an auto plant used by auto workers to make automobiles. Both are good illustrations. But capital is also education used by a person to improve his or her skills. This type of capital is called human capital. It serves the same function as a plough or auto plant, but is not as visible.

What's labor? A resource that represents the physical and intellectual effort of people engaged in the activity of producing goods and services. Economists are careful to differentiate between labor that people freely sell for a specified period of time in return for a wage or salary, and labor that is extracted by coercion. In the first case, the person working is the decision maker; in the latter case, the person is subjected to someone else's decision making. Is slave labor really labor?

What's capital? Economists identify capital, not by form or substance, but by purpose. The purpose of a plough is to produce the food we eat. We don't eat ploughs. The purpose of live bait (little fish) is to produce the bigger fish we eat. We don't eat bait. In other words, capital represents a resource whose purpose it is to produce other goods we consume.

What's land? Land is a gift of nature. Nobody actually produces it. Think of an untouched field. Once put to production, its purpose is to produce goods. The basic difference between capital and land is that capital is manufactured—a hammer, a freight train—while land is natural. It is referred to as a natural resource. But once the land is improved—cleared for cultivation, pesticides, herbicides, and fertilizer applied—it becomes a mixture or combination of land and capital.

Entrepreneurship is a treasured resource in our market economy. The entrepreneur is the person who puts it all together. The entrepreneur conceives of the business's essential idea, decides what resources to use and how to use them, markets the goods produced, and reaps the rewards (or failures) associated with the business venture. The entrepreneur alone assumes the risks of uncertainty that are inherent in any business undertaking.

With these concepts understood, the chapter analyzes the production possibilities of a simple economy. To make it as simple as possible, we set the economy on an island and the resources consist of one person—Robinson Crusoe—and the natural resources of the island. It is really sufficient to show the many complexities of modern economies.

Robinson Crusoe spends his waking day producing consumer goods and/or capital goods. Table 1 in the text outlines his production possibilities. If he chooses to produce only consumption goods, he can produce six. If he chooses to produce one unit of capital, he can only produce five consumption goods. A simple set of options, and enough for economists to explain one of the most fundamental concepts in economics: Cost. Economists refer to cost as opportunity cost because it is defined as the quantities of a good that must be given up in order to produce a unit of another good. In this case, one consumption good was sacrificed in order to produce one capital good. The opportunity cost of the first unit of capital, then, is one unit of consumption.

If Robinson Crusoe decides to produce two units of capital, he discovers that he can only produce three units of consumption. In other words, the opportunity cost of the second unit of capital is two units of consumption. Note what's happening. As more capital goods are being produced, the opportunity cost associated with each additional unit increases. This phenomenon is explained by the fact that resources are not of equal quality and is described as the law of increasing costs.

Why would Robinson Crusoe consider producing capital goods? He is a person with foresight. He knows that adding capital to his resource stock—he has labor and land—will allow him to produce more later on. The more ingredients, the bigger the cake. Look at the following figure.

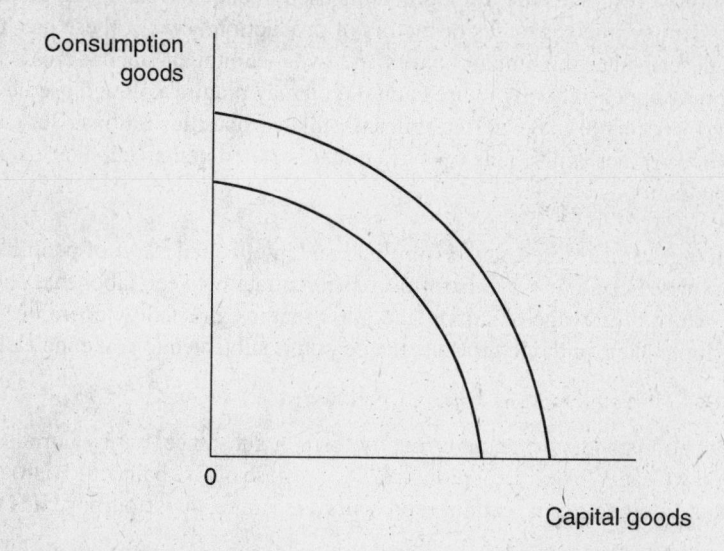

The production possibilities curve bows out from the origin reflecting the law of increasing cost. As resources grow—in this case, more and more capital added to Robinson Crusoe's resource stock—the curve shifts out to the right. In time, with Crusoe's capital increasing, he can produce more consumption goods than he did at the beginning of the story and still keep producing more capital. In simple terms, the rich get richer.

We can use this simple Robinson Crusoe model of production possibilities to generalize about modern economies today. Economies that focus on producing capital goods set themselves up for more capital and consumption goods in the future. Capital goods production is the wellspring of economic growth and society's economic betterment. If economies consume most of what they produce—as many poor economies do today—they forfeit the chance to grow. Economic betterment is pushed aside. It is even possible for economies to shrink—if they eat into their meager capital stock—and they become worse off tomorrow than they are today.

Innovations play a decisive role in production. They represent new technologies. The chapter describes how Robinson Crusoe builds a fishing net to replace the fishing spear. The net technology allows him to produce more goods with the same quantity of resources. Compare jet aircraft to wooden ships crossing the Atlantic!

Wars cause production possibilities curves to collapse inward. A nation's capital stock, which may have taken decades to develop, can be ruined in a matter of days. People, too, are its victims. However devastating a war can be to an economy, it is not unusual for nations, who have suffered severe physical and human loss to war, to quickly

CHAPTER 2   PRODUCTION POSSIBILITIES AND OPPORTUNITY COSTS   THE BASICS   13

rebound in the post-war years. The explanation for such recovery, Japan and Germany are notable examples, is that ideas and technological knowledge are indestructible.

Production possibilities curves identify unemployment. When an economy operates on its production possibilities curve, it implies that all resources are fully employed. Unemployment exists when the economy operates at some point within the curve. The opportunity cost of producing more goods under conditions of unemployment is zero. After all, no resources need to be shifted away from goods being produced. With idle resources available, nothing need be sacrificed.

The chapter concludes with a discussion of division of labor and specialization. Economists have noted—as early as Adam Smith's *Wealth of Nations* in 1776—that if people were allowed to specialize in the work they do, they become more expert at what they do, more productive doing it, and in the end, the total output produced by everyone increases.

Key Terms — Test your comprehension by defining and explaining the significance of these terms.

factors of production	opportunity cost
labor	law of increasing costs
capital	vicious circle of poverty
human capital	innovation
land	underemployed resources
entrepreneur	economic efficiency
production possibilities	labor specialization

True-False Questions — If a statement is false, explain why.

1. Factors of production include consumer goods. (T/F)

2. When I vacuum my home, I perform labor that economists regard as a factor of production. (T/F)

3. When my hired housekeeper vacuums my home, he is performing labor. (T/F)

4. Capital is a good used to produce or market another good. (T/F)

5. Personal computers are considered capital goods because they are so expensive. (T/F)

6. Entrepreneurs share the risks and uncertainties of business ventures with all other factors of production. (T/F)

7. The opportunity cost of a bushel of wheat is the money that must be sacrificed in order to produce it. (T/F)

8. An economy that operates along its production possibilities frontier is economically efficient. (T/F)

9. The production possibilities for an economy expand as the quantities of the economy's resources increase. (T/F)

10. The production possibilities frontiers for all economies always shift to the right. (T/F)

11. A production possibilities frontier that is a straight line reflects the law of increasing costs. (T/F)

12. The richer the economy, the more easily it can grow because the proportion of its resources needed to produce consumption goods becomes smaller. (T/F)

13. An economy that has some underemployed resources can still operate on its production possibilities frontier. (T/F)

14. In Adam Smith's pin factory example, workers were each given a very simple task to perform in producing pins because the process was technologically backward. (T/F)

15. Only poor economies, whose resources and technologies are limited, face production possibilities curves. (T/F)

Multiple Choice Questions

1. Lumber, used in the production of a farmer's barn, is
   a. a consumption good because the farmer will use the barn.
   b. a land resource because it is the product of a tree.
   c. capital because it is a good used to make other goods.
   d. human capital because it contains labor which made the lumber from the tree.
   e. neither a consumption good nor a factor of production because it is raw material.

2. Points A and B on the production possibilities frontier shown here represent combinations in country A and country B, respectively. These positions suggest that in the future
   a. country A will grow much faster than country B.
   b. country B will grow much faster than country A.
   c. country A will grow very slowly because its population lacks consumer goods.
   d. country B is less prepared to produce for the future than country A.
   e. both countries have unemployed resources.

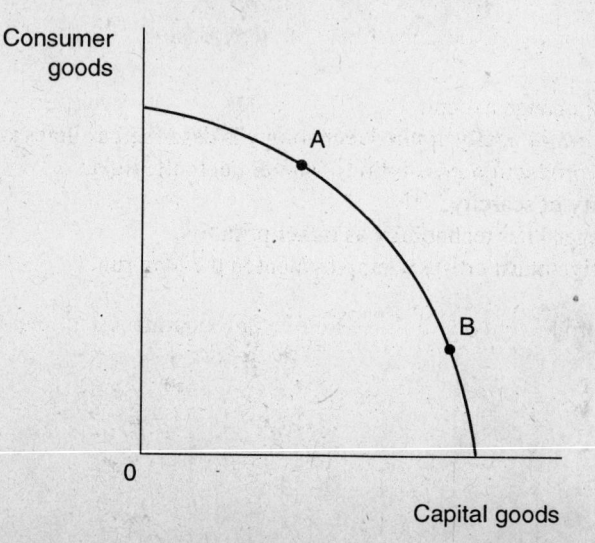

3. The production possibilities model applies
   a. only to economies that produce simple goods, like the illustrated Crusoe economy.
   b. to economies without labor specialization.
   c. to economies without division of labor.
   d. to economies whose factors of production are fully employed.
   e. universally, to all economies regardless of their differences.

4. If an economy experiences unemployment, it would show up as a point
   a. on the production possibilities curve but on one of the axes.
   b. outside the production possibilities frontier.
   c. inside the production possibilities frontier.
   d. on the production possibilities frontier.
   e. on a production possibilities frontier that is shifting to the right.

5. The opportunity cost of producing a good is
   a. the amount paid in dollar terms.
   b. the quantity of other goods that must be sacrificed in order to produce the good.
   c. impossible to compute in most cases because it is a model concept.
   d. an important accounting concept that economists borrow to explain value.
   e. higher than most people realize because scarce resources are expensive.

6. The law of increasing cost suggests all of the following except that
   a. resources, such as labor and land, are not of equal quality or fertility.
   b. resources, such as labor and land, are of equal quality and fertility.
   c. switching from producing one good to another involves increasing sacrifices of the first good.
   d. opportunity cost of producing a good is not constant along a bowed-out production possibilities curve.
   e. resources are not interchangeable between productive activities.

7. To economists, the term "capital" refers exclusively to
   a. goods used to produce other goods.
   b. money used to purchase stocks and bonds.
   c. savings accumulated by households to purchase real estate.
   d. money used by a capitalist to hire workers.
   e. machinery used by workers to produce goods.

8. An entrepreneur is a person who
   a. earns incomes higher than those earned by workers.
   b. is a hired manager.
   c. assumes all the risks and rewards associated with a business venture.
   d. buys and sells stocks and bonds.
   e. hires and fires workers.

9. The following is true of technological change except:
   a. an idea that eventually takes the form of newly applied technology is described as innovation.
   b. technological change can shift the production possibilities frontier out to the right.
   c. new technology reduces the severity of scarcity.
   d. our grandchildren will no doubt regard our technology as rather primitive.
   e. new technology, although productive, must create unemployment in the long run.

10. Capital accumulation or formation in an economy occurs when
    a. more inputs are used in production.
    b. resources are shifted from the production of consumer goods to the production of capital goods.
    c. new technologies are adopted.
    d. workers work longer hours.
    e. the economy operates at full employment.

11. One of the reasons that poor economies tend to stay poor is that
    a. workers in these economies are not sufficiently motivated.
    b. their governments overtax business profit.
    c. most of the resources are devoted to consumer goods production so little capital accumulation occurs.
    d. they are exploited by the industrially advanced economies.
    e. they follow failed socialist policies.

12. If an economy is operating along its production possibilities frontier, then it is clear that
    a. all factors of production are fully employed.
    b. poverty has likely been eliminated.
    c. rapid technological change is easiest to achieve.
    d. some resources may still be underemployed.
    e. economic growth must slow down.

13. The most likely explanation for the shift in the production possibilities frontier shown here is
    a. a decrease in the supplies of some inputs.
    b. a decrease in the supplies of all inputs.
    c. the adoption by the government of a full employment policy.
    d. a shift out of capital goods to consumer goods production.
    e. simultaneous technological advance in the two sectors.

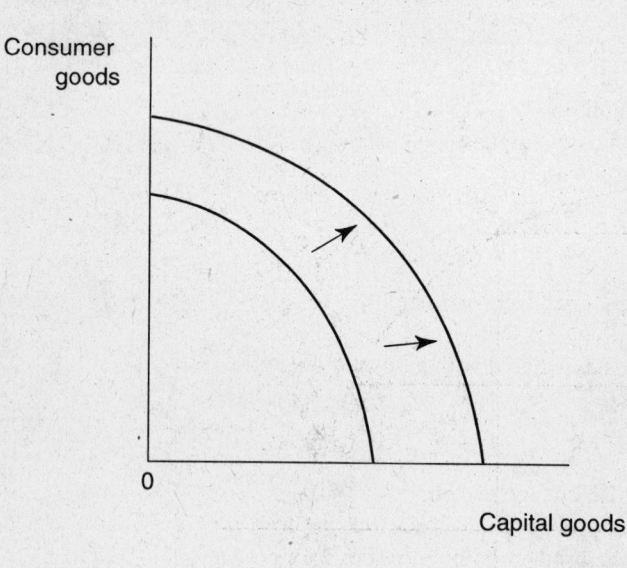

14. An entrepreneur _____ the manager of a business enterprise who assumes _____ for the success or failure of the enterprise.
    a. is always; no responsibility
    b. may or may not be; full responsibility
    c. cannot be; full responsibility
    d. desires to be; full responsibility
    e. is; partial responsibility

CHAPTER 2   PRODUCTION POSSIBILITIES AND OPPORTUNITY COSTS   THE BASICS   17

15. All of the following are capital goods except:
    a. the lawnmower in your garage used to cut your grass.
    b. the movie theater in the mall that features first-run movies.
    c. the concession stand at Pittsburgh's Riverfront Stadium where the Pirates play baseball.
    d. the card tables at a gambling casino.
    e. a scuba instructor's scuba gear.

16. All of the following represent examples of underemployment except:
    a. a cab driver who has a Ph.D. in computer science, but can't get a job in computer science.
    b. a victim of race discrimination who is denied entry into a chosen profession.
    c. a young woman denied promotion only because she lacked seniority.
    d. a young woman denied promotion only because she is a woman.
    e. a young woman with a Ph.D. who is now a full-time mother of three children.

17. To hire resources, such as land, labor, or capital, a buyer must be willing to pay an amount
    a. at least equal to the resource's opportunity cost.
    b. less than the resource's opportunity cost, to make a profit.
    c. more than the resource's opportunity cost, to attract the resource into employment.
    d. that the owner of the resource demands.
    e. that eliminates the underemployment of the resource.

18. Given the following production possibilities frontier, the cost of increasing capital goods production from one to two is
    a. five consumption goods.
    b. four consumption goods.
    c. three consumption goods.
    d. two consumption goods.
    e. one consumption good.

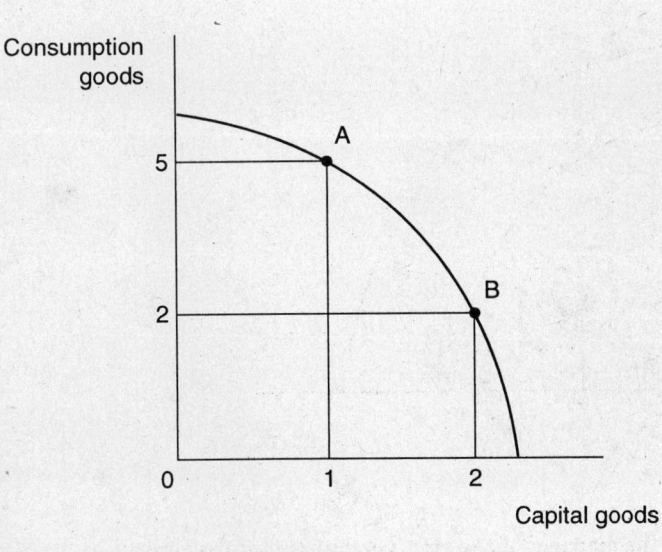

19. Suppose an economy shifts resources from the production of guns to butter, and for an additional unit of butter produced must give up greater amounts of guns. Which of the following statements cannot be true?
    a. The law of increasing costs does not apply.
    b. The production possibilities frontier is bowed out.
    c. The shape of the production possibilities frontier remains unchanged.
    d. The opportunity cost of butter calculated in terms of guns sacrificed increases.
    e. Resources continue to be specialized.

20. An economy that is efficient will
    a. produce combinations of goods that lie beyond (to the right of) its production possibilities frontier.
    b. produce combinations of goods that lie within (to the left of) its production possibilities frontier.
    c. produce combinations of goods that are always consistent with full employment.
    d. sacrifice unemployment for underemployment.
    e. create employment that guarantees above poverty-level incomes for its citizens.

Questions for Discussion

1. Does my son pulling weeds in the backyard at my command constitute labor? Does your answer change if my son and I agree that he will be paid $0.25 per bucket of weeds pulled? Explain.

2. What is the opportunity cost of your college education? How does the opportunity cost change if you benefit from a generous federally sponsored tuition grant? Can you make an argument in favor of federal tuition grants?

CHAPTER 2   PRODUCTION POSSIBILITIES AND OPPORTUNITY COSTS   THE BASICS   19

3. Why do most people specialize?

4. How does the law of increasing costs affect China's ability to take advantage of opportunities for specialization and division of labor that a large population size affords? To answer, you may want to use the following production possibilities curve where China's economy is depicted producing food and manufactured (nonfood) goods. What happens as China attempts to move from point A to point B?

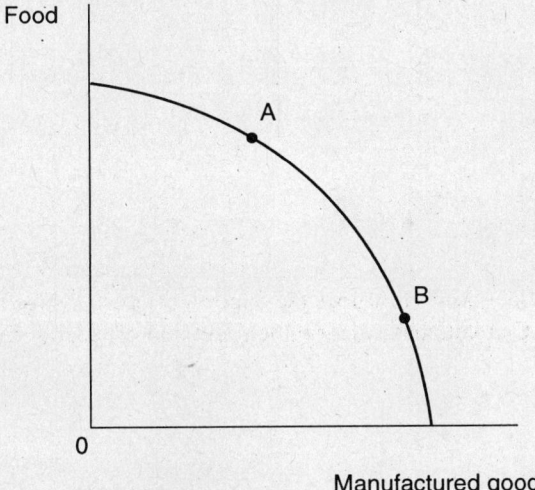

Problems

1. Suppose that an economy's resources are unspecialized so that its resources can be shifted from one production process to another without experiencing increasing costs. How would this country's production possibilities curve be shaped? Draw the production possibilities curve and explain the shape.

2. How does a production possibilities curve shift as a result of an increase in the stock of capital that can be used in either production process?

Answers to Questions

True-False Questions

1. False because consumer goods are part of the goods and services that factors of production produce.
2. False unless someone agreed to pay me for cleaning my own house.
3. True
4. True
5. False because expense has nothing to do with whether a good is capital or not.
6. False because an entrepreneur is completely responsible for the business's success or failure.
7. False because the opportunity cost is the amount of other goods that must be given up to produce the bushel of wheat.
8. True
9. True
10. False because growth isn't guaranteed for an economy.
11. False because only bowed-out curves depict the law of increasing costs.
12. True
13. False because full employment of all resources in the economy is a requirement for its being on the curve.
14. False because the simple tasks reflect division of labor which is responsible for increases in productivity.
15. False because scarcity characterizes all societies.

Multiple Choice Questions

1. c	6. a	11. c	16. e
2. b	7. a	12. a	17. a
3. e	8. c	13. e	18. c
4. c	9. e	14. b	19. a
5. b	10. b	15. a	20. c

Questions for Discussion

1. My son will tell you that the only way he will pull weeds in the backyard without pay is if I coerce him to do so. If we agree that he will be paid, then the work is labor.

2. The opportunity cost of going to college is the dollar cost plus whatever amount you could have made in a job. The opportunity cost is lowered by the grant.

3. People tend to specialize in what they do best relative to others because they realize the highest labor productivity this way. High labor productivity translates into relatively high wages.

4. Because China's population is so large, many people must be involved in the production of food just to keep the people above starvation levels. The law of increasing costs sets in as the more specialized (and more productive) food producers are moved into the production of manufactured goods.

Problems

1. This country's production possibilities curve would be a straight line. Resources could be shifted from one good to another at a constant opportunity cost.

2. The production possibilities curve shifts out, the shift depending on where the resources are placed.

CHAPTER 3

DEMAND AND SUPPLY

Chapter Summary

How are prices determined? This is the basic question we explore in this chapter. Let's conclude before we start our analysis of price determination: Price depends on demand and supply. That's it. But what's demand and what's supply?

Demand represents people's willingness to buy goods and services. The price of the good, say a T-shirt, measures just how willing people are to buy the good. We measure a person's demand for T-shirts by relating specific quantities of T-shirts the person will buy at *specific prices*. What happens to quantity demanded when price falls? It increases. This inverse relationship between quantity demanded and price is called the law of demand. When the price of gasoline falls, the quantity of gasoline demanded increases. When the price of health care goes up, the quantity of health care demanded falls. You behave that way with respect to demand, your friends behave that way, and your professor behaves that way. Market demand versus individual demand? The market demand for T-shirts is simply the sum of all individual demands. Make up a table showing market demand for T-shirts. Draw the appropriate demand curve.

What about supply? Supply represents a producer's willingness to supply goods at specific prices. The analysis of supply is a little more complicated than the illustration of the law of demand. Although quantity supplied depends upon price—that's like demand—*it also depends upon time*. Producers need time to adjust their ability to supply goods to their willingness to supply them. For example, if I offered you $500 for a dozen roses *now*, you would be willing, but unable to supply them. If I gave you ample time, you could and would supply. Economists differentiate between market-day supply, short-run supply, and long-run supply. The differentiating factor is time. We saw that in our fishing illustration. In market-day supply, the quantity supplied remains unchanged regardless of price (no ability whatsoever to change quantity supplied, even if you'd love to). The relationship between price and quantity supplied in the short-run is positive—higher prices, more quantity supplied—but there are limits to how much quantity supplied can change in the short run. Again, remember the fishing illustration. You can load up the boat you are using—more crew, more equipment—but you can't enlarge your boat or add a second one that quickly. That takes more time. Long-run supply reflects that more time. It represents the situation in which you are actually able to produce what you're willing to produce at various prices. Economists formalize the differences in supply by noting that all productive resources are variable in long-run supply, at least one isn't variable in short-run supply, and none are variable in market-day supply. Look at the text to compare how these supply curves are drawn.

Let's bring people's willingness to demand T-shirts at various prices and producers' willingness to supply T-shirts (let's use the short-run) at various prices together in the T-shirt market. The result: Equilibrium price and quantities bought and sold. If price is above its equilibrium level, excess supply will create competition among sellers to drive price down. If price is below equilibrium, competition among demanders will drive price up. Either way, we end up in equilibrium.

Let's now consider shifts in demand and supply curves and show how they influence equilibrium price. We start with demand. Imagine a market demand curve for T-shirts where at a price of $10, quantity demanded is 4,000. Now suppose next week, at the same price of $10, quantity demanded increases to 5,000. What could explain the *change in demand?* Perhaps tastes for T-shirts changed. It became more stylish. Or incomes increased. Or the price of other goods—dress shirts and polo shirts—increased. Or more people are in the market. Or people expect the price of T-shirts to increase next week. Each of these factors can explain why, at every price, quantity demanded will increase. Note the difference between a change in quantity demanded—movement along a demand curve—and a change in demand—an actual shift in the demand curve. If the demand curve shifts out to the right—and assuming no change in the supply curve—a new and higher equilibrium price results.

CHAPTER 3 DEMAND AND SUPPLY   THE BASICS   23

What about a change in supply? Changes in technology, in resource prices, in the price of other goods, and in the number of suppliers can change supply. If the supply curve increases—a shift in the supply curve out to the right—and assuming no change in the demand curve, a new and lower equilibrium price results.

If the demand curve and the supply curve change at the same time, then equilibrium price will change, its direction depending upon the strength of the changes in demand and supply. Look at the illustration in the text and try a few out on your own. Make some minor changes and some major ones and compare the results to those in the text.

Economists describe price as a rationing function. Here's why. If the price of a Broadway musical is $300 for a balcony seat, you don't go. It's either too expensive (students' incomes are typically low) or your taste for musicals is not that keen. Either way, you don't go. But Donald Trump might. He doesn't blink at a $300 price, and he may really enjoy the show. The point is: There are only so many seats. Some go, some don't. Who decides? Price does. Price is the rationing mechanism. It weeds out those who are unwilling to pay $300—for whatever reason—for the seat.

Key Terms — Test your comprehension by defining and explaining the significance of these terms.

change in quantity demanded	excess demand
law of demand	equilibrium price
demand schedule	short run
demand curve	long run
market demand	change in demand
supply schedule	normal good
market-day supply	substitute goods
supply curve	complementary goods
excess supply	change in supply

True-False Questions — If a statement is false, explain why.

1. The law of demand suggests that as price decreases quantity demanded decreases. (T/F)

2. A demand schedule shows people's willingness to buy specific quantities of a good at specific prices. (T/F)

3. An individual demand curve is identical to the market demand curve in a particular market. (T/F)

4. The market demand curve is downward sloping. (T/F)

5. A supply schedule depends upon the willingness of demanders to buy the quantities supplied at various prices. (T/F)

6. Market-day supply is unchangeable except in emergency situations such as food supply in a famine relief effort. (T/F)

7. Excess demand exists only when price is below its equilibrium level. (T/F)

8. When price is at its equilibrium level, the quantity demanded is equal to quantity supplied. (T/F)

9. An increase in supply will create a new lower equilibrium price and an excess demand at the original price. (T/F)

10. A decrease in supply will create a new higher equilibrium price and an excess demand at the original price. (T/F)

11. Excess supply can only arise if the price is below the equilibrium price. (T/F)

12. If the price of one good increases and the demand for another good increases as a result, then the goods must be substitutes. (T/F)

13. If the price of one good decreases and the demand for another good increases as a result, then the goods must be complements. (T/F)

14. If a supplier is only able to partially adjust quantity supplied to a change in price, then the supply curve must be short run. (T/F)

15. The long run is a time period sufficient to allow suppliers to make most of the changes necessary to adjust the quantity supplied to price changes. (T/F)

16. A change in demand refers to a movement along a demand curve but change in quantity demanded refers to a shift in the entire demand curve. (T/F)

17. An increase in income will usually result in an increase in demand for a good. (T/F)

Multiple-Choice Questions

1. If a market is in equilibrium, then
   a. demand curves and supply curves are the same.
   b. at the equilibrium price, quantity supplied is equal to quantity demanded.
   c. the short run quantities of supply and demand equal long run quantities of supply and demand.
   d. the short-run equilibrium price equals the long-run equilibrium price.
   e. all demanders receive the goods they want, all suppliers sell the goods they want.

2. If excess demand exists in a market, then
   a. excess supply will emerge to absorb the excess demand.
   b. quantity supplied is less than the quantity demanded.
   c. quantity demanded is less than quantity supplied.
   d. equilibrium price is below the market price.
   e. market price will fall.

CHAPTER 3 DEMAND AND SUPPLY

3. Market demand for fish represents
   a. the sum of all individual demands for fish.
   b. the specific quantities consumers will buy, given the market-day supply.
   c. the relationship between price and quantity of fish demanded by a consumer on the fish market.
   d. the maximum quantity consumers will buy, given the limitations of their income.
   e. the reciprocal of the market supply of fish.

4. An increase in demand will result in
   a. an increase in supply as new firms enter the market.
   b. an increase in price and an increase in supply.
   c. an increase in price and an increase in quantity supplied.
   d. a decrease in demand in the future.
   e. a decrease in price and an increase in quantity supplied.

5. If supply increases and demand does not change, then
   a. price as well as quantity demanded and supplied will increase.
   b. price will decrease and quantity demanded and supplied will increase.
   c. price will decrease and quantity demanded and supplied will decrease.
   d. price and quantity demanded remain unchanged.
   e. price remains unchanged, but both quantity demanded and supplied will decrease.

6. This graph shows
   a. a market-day supply curve.
   b. a short-run supply curve.
   c. that suppliers will supply as much as their capacities allow, given a specific price.
   d. that suppliers will supply as much as their capacities allow, given changes in price.
   e. suppliers who do not respond to price changes.

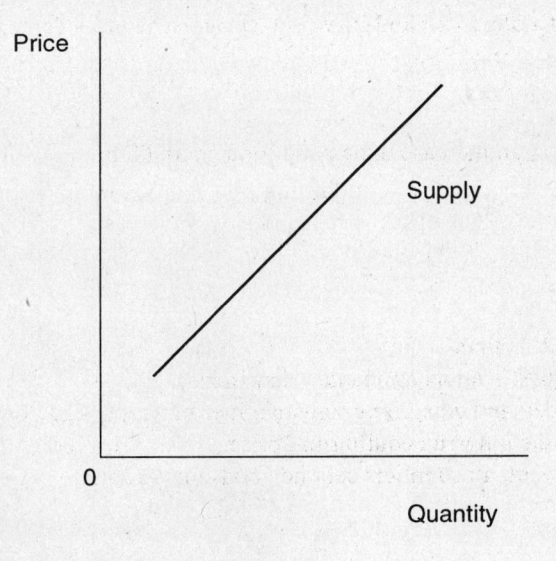

7. If, at a specific price, quantity demanded is greater than the quantity supplied, then
   a. the market clears, although some demanders cannot completely satisfy their demands.
   b. price will decrease until the excess supply is eliminated.
   c. price will increase until the excess demand is eliminated.
   d. price will remain unchanged since the market will clear at that price.
   e. price will decrease and quantity supplied will increase.

8. Suppose there is a widespread rumor that Japanese car manufacturers plan next month to increase the price of their cars by 50 percent; you would expect that in the U.S., the demand curve for Japanese cars
   a. would shift to the left next month.
   b. would shift to the right next month.
   c. would shift to the right before next month.
   d. would shift to the left before next month.
   e. would remains unchanged, but the price of U.S. cars would decrease next month.

9. The basic difference between the short run and the long run is that
   a. in the short run, suppliers cannot adjust output to changes in demand.
   b. in the long run, suppliers can make any necessary adjustments to output.
   c. in the short run, a new business can enter an industry.
   d. in the short run, failing businesses must close.
   e. in the long run, demanders can adjust their demands to their incomes.

10. When economists refer to price as a rationing mechanism, they mean
    a. that the government can set up a rationing program by setting prices.
    b. that price weeds out those from the market who want the good, but can't afford it.
    c. that most markets have chronic problems with excess demand so rationing is necessary.
    d. that suppliers ration goods by setting a price demanders can afford.
    e. that demanders ration their incomes by choosing only those prices that suppliers can meet.

11. Which of the following will not cause a change in demand for a particular good?
    a. a change in the price of a related good
    b. a change in income
    c. a change in tastes
    d. a change in expectations about future prices
    e. a change in the price of the good

12. When the market price is higher than its equilibrium level, we can expect that
    a. as the equilibrium price rises, the quantity supplied will increase.
    b. as the equilibrium price rises, the quantity demanded will decrease.
    c. the quantity supplied and demanded will both fall as equilibrium price adjusts to market price.
    d. the quantity supplied and demanded will both rise as equilibrium price adjusts to market price.
    e. as market price falls to its equilibrium level, the quantity demanded will increase.

13. Consider the market shown in the following graph. A change in price from $10 to $8 results in
    a. a decrease in demand.
    b. an increase in demand.
    c. an increase in demand and a decrease in quantity supplied.
    d. an increase in quantity demanded.
    e. a decrease in quantity demanded.

CHAPTER 3 DEMAND AND SUPPLY

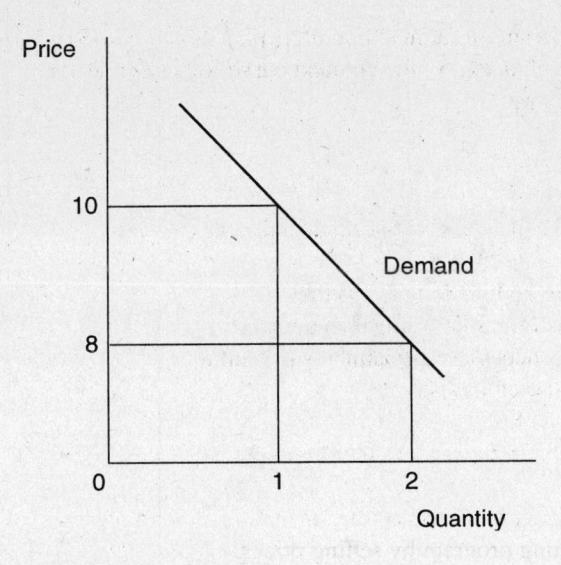

14. In the previous graph, the downward-sloping demand curve illustrates the
    a. law of demand.
    b. impact of the *ceteris paribus* assumption.
    c. decrease in demand that results when price falls.
    d. increase in demand that results when price falls.
    e. excess demand that results when price falls.

15. If consumers are presented with hard scientific evidence that a diet of moderate red wine consumption and pate de foie gras leads to lower rates of heart disease, which of the following changes is likely to occur?
    a. an increase in red wine prices
    b. an increase in white wine prices
    c. an increase in brie cheese prices
    d. a decrease in grape prices
    e. an increase in beer prices

16. Consider the two supply curves shown in the following graph. The most likely conclusion you draw is that
    a. S is the short-run curve, while S' is the long-run curve.
    b. S is the long-run curve, while S' is the short-run curve.
    c. S is the market-day curve, while S' is either short-run or long-run.
    d. Both curves represent market-day supply, but in two different markets.
    e. S is either short-run or market-day, while S' is the long-run.

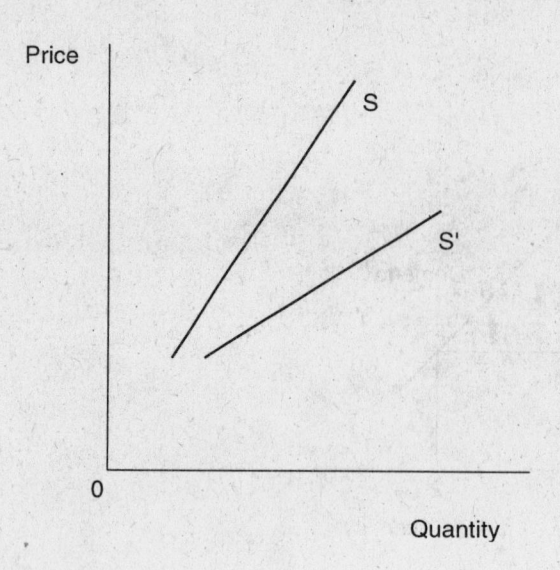

17. Which of the following will not cause a change in the supply of pencils?
    a. a change in pencil-making technology
    b. a change in resources prices associated with pencil making
    c. a change in the price of pens and other substitute goods
    d. a change in the price of pencils
    e. a change in the number of pencil suppliers

18. Suppose the demand and supply for strawberries decrease, but the decrease in demand is major while the increase in supply is minor. Under these conditions
    a. price increases and quantity demanded and supplied decrease.
    b. price decreases and quantity demanded and supplied increase.
    c. price decreases and quantity demanded and supplied decreases.
    d. price increases and quantity demanded and supplied increase.
    e. price remains unchanged, but quantity demanded and supplied decrease.

19. Suppose that the demand and supply for computers grow. The price of computers should
    a. decrease, if the increase in supply is more prominent than the increase in demand.
    b. decrease, if the increase in demand is more prominent than the increase in supply.
    c. increase, if the increase in supply is more prominent than the increase in demand.
    d. increase, if the decrease in demand is more prominent than the increase in supply.
    e. remain unchanged since demand and supply both increased.

20. A change in quantity demanded always results from
    a. a change in tastes.
    b. a change in price.
    c. a change in income.
    d. a change in the price of substitutes.
    e. a change in the price of complements.

Problems

1. The following table shows the demand and supply schedules for an initial release of the first compact disc by the new all-female hip-hop group Girlz to Womyn.

Price ($/disc)	Quantity Demanded	Quantity Supplied
$20	40,000	100,000
18	60,000	100,000
16	80,000	100,000
14	100,000	100,000
12	120,000	100,000
10	140,000	100,000

   a. On the grid, carefully plot the demand curve and the supply curve.

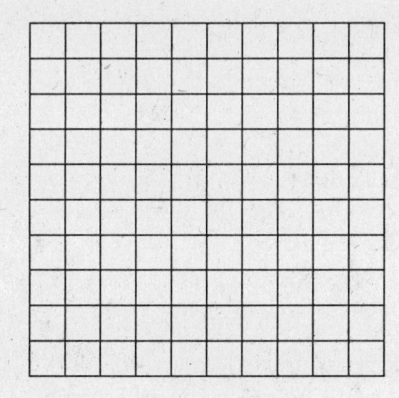

   b. What time frame is represented by the supply curve you have drawn? How do you know?

   c. What is the equilibrium price, quantity demanded, and quantity supplied?

   d. At each price listed in the table, note whether an excess demand or supply exists and its magnitude.

   e. Suppose that record executives had initially issued 120,000 compact discs for Girlz to Womyn's first album. Show this new supply on the grid and explain how the answers to parts c and d above would change.

Discussion Questions

1. Richard III was willing to exchange his kingdom for a horse. What was the opportunity cost of his not having a horse?

2. Why are demand curves downward sloping?

3. Explain the difference between changes in quantity demanded and changes in demand.

4. Would the following events cause a change in demand or a change in quantity demanded in the market for automobiles? Explain.

   a. A limit is placed on the number of cars that can be imported from Japan.

   b. Malaysia becomes a major new exporter of cars to the United States.

   c. Congress passes a big tax increase in an attempt to deal with the deficit.

   d. A report is issued suggesting that air travel has become much less safe in recent years.

   e. The legal driving age is lowered to 15.

5. Draw market-day, the short-run, and the long-run supply curves. Why do the slopes of these supply curves differ?

CHAPTER 3 DEMAND AND SUPPLY

6. The sketch shows the market for apples after the announcement that the chemical Alar, used to control the rate at which apples ripen, may pose a health threat. The demand curve shifts to the left, from D to D'. Starting at the original price, explain step-by-step how the new equilibrium price is reached.

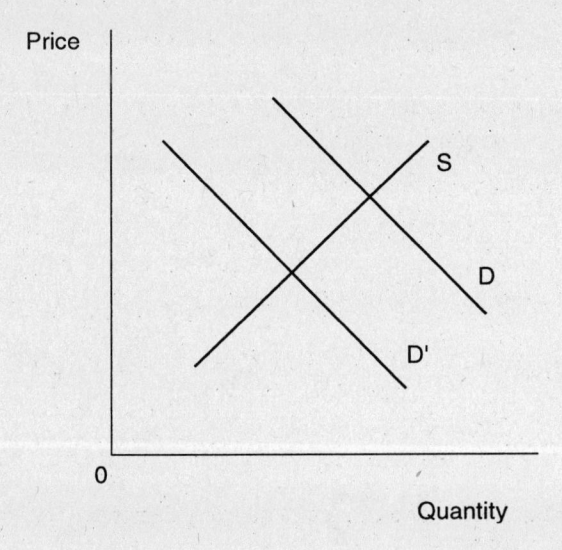

Answers to Questions

True-False Questions

1. False because quantity demand increases as price decreases.
2. True
3. False because individual demand is one person's demand.
4. True
5. False because the supply curve merely shows the relationship between price and quantity supplied.
6. False because market day supply means that suppliers cannot change quantity supplied by definition.
7. True
8. True
9. False because an increase in supply will create an excess supply at the original price.
10. True
11. False because an excess supply requires that price be above equilibrium.
12. True
13. True
14. True
15. False because the long run allows suppliers to make all changes necessary.
16. False because a change in demand is a shift in the curve and a change in quantity demand is a shift along the curve due to a price change.
17. True

Multiple Choice Questions

1. b	6. b	11. e	16. a
2. b	7. c	12. e	17. d
3. a	8. c	13. d	18. a
4. c	9. b	14. a	19. a
5. b	10. b	15. a	20. b

Problem

1. a. See the diagram.

Supply and Demand for Girlz to Womyn

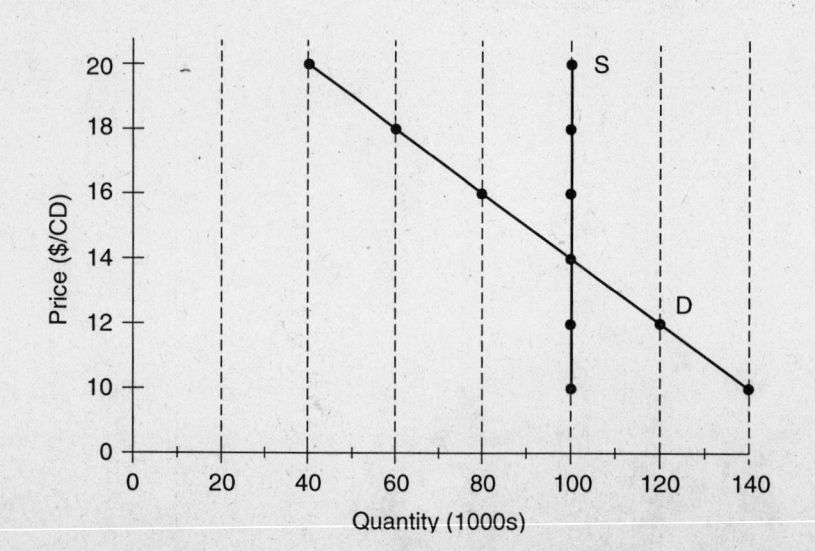

b. The market day because the supply curve is vertical.

c. The equilibrium price is $14 and quantity demanded equals quantity supplied at 100,000 CDs.

d. At $20, excess supply equals 60,000.
   At $18, excess supply equals 40,000.
   At $16, excess supply equals 20,000.
   At $12, excess demand equals 20,000.
   At $10, excess demand equals 40,000.

e. The new supply curve could be represented by a vertical line drawn at 120,000. The new equilibrium price is $12. Subtract quantity demanded from 120,000 to find excess supply or demand at each price.

Discussion Questions

1. The opportunity cost of not having a horse was his kingdom. Prices represent opportunity costs to individuals who pay them.

2. Think of a good on sale. If the good is marked down by 25 percent, wouldn't you expect more units to be demanded? It seems logical and our experience confirms it. Economists say that the marked-down price—assuming other prices remain unchanged—makes the good more attractive than other goods and we switch from other goods to it.

3. A change in demand is a shift in the entire curve and a change in quantity demanded is a shift along the curve.

4. a. a change in quantity demand since price will go up
   b. a change in quantity demand since the supply curve shifts
   c. a change in demand since incomes will change
   d. a change in demand since tastes about driving compared to flying will change
   e. a change in demand since the number of drivers will change

5. Your drawing should show a vertical supply curve in the market day and a steeper supply curve for the short run than for the long run. The shapes differ because with greater time suppliers have greater flexibility adjusting to price changes.

6. After the shift in demand at the original price, an excess supply will exist, causing price to fall. It will keep falling until quantity demanded equals quantity supplied at a new and lower equilibrium price. There, quantity demanded and supplied will be less than the original quantities.

CHAPTER 4

AGGREGATE DEMAND AND AGGREGATE SUPPLY

Chapter Summary

Gross domestic product (GDP) is the term economists use to describe an economy's total output. It is defined as the total value of all final goods and services, measured in current market prices, produced in the economy during a year. The qualifier "final goods" means that GDP does not include goods that are used to produce other goods in that year. For example, 1996 GDP includes the value of a table produced in July, but not the value of the lumber, produced in March, to make that table. A fuller discussion of GDP awaits us in the following chapter.

1996 GDP may be larger than 1995 GDP but less than 1997 GDP. Each year, the value of the economy's output changes. Economists identify a pattern associated with these output changes which they describe as the business cycle. Look at the following figure.

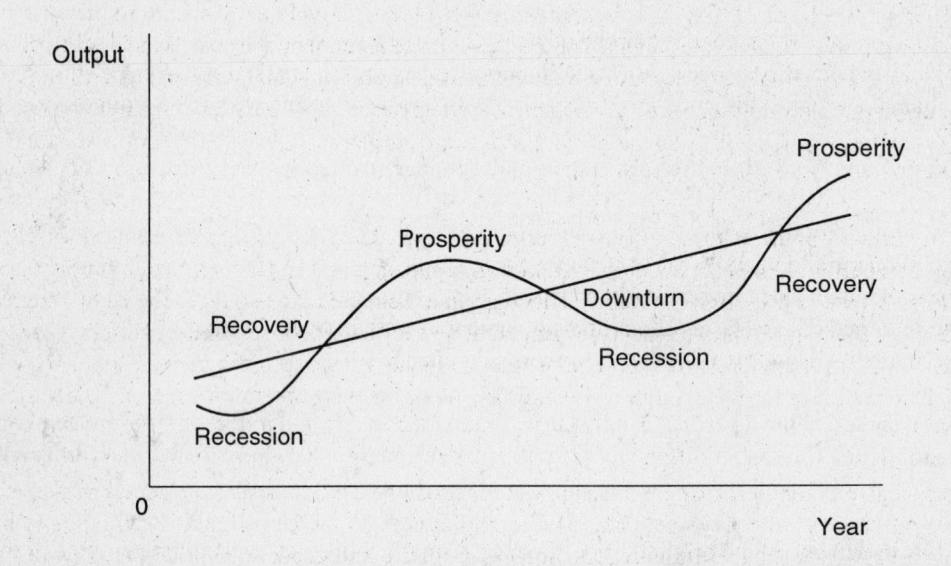

Note that the cycle runs through four phases: recession, recovery, prosperity, and downturn. Then it's back to recession and the cycle repeats. Note also the upward tilt of the cycle. The economy's output in the second prosperity phase is greater than output in the preceding prosperity phase. The slope of the trend line shown in the figure reflects the economy's rate of economic growth.

Economists distinguish between real and nominal GDP. Suppose 1994 GDP was $100 and 1995 GDP was $200. Does that mean twice as many final goods and services were produced in 1995? Not necessarily. What if all prices doubled in 1995 so that a loaf of bread priced at $0.75 in 1994 is priced at $1.50 in 1995? The value of the output (bread) doubled, but the quantity of bread remains the same. No *real* change, right? Well, what can we say about that $200 GDP in 1995? Is it really twice the 1994 GDP? It depends on whether prices changed and by how much. Economists use the GDP deflator (at times, the consumer price index and others) to record price changes. The GDP deflator compares the prices of all goods and services in a year to the prices in a base year. If the 1995 GDP deflator is 125 (with 1994 as base year), then $40 of the $100 increase in 1995 GDP is accounted for by price increases, while $60 of that $100 increase represents real goods and services. We read: Nominal GDP for 1995 is $200, but real GDP is $160.

34

But why are prices what they are and why is GDP what it is? The aggregate demand and aggregate supply model allows us to explore how the equilibrium level of real GDP and the price level are determined. Aggregate supply measures the total quantity of goods and services that firms in the economy are willing to supply at varying price levels. Aggregate demand measures the total quantity of goods and services demanded by households, firms, foreigners, and government at varying price levels.

The aggregate supply curve has three distinct segments: horizontal, upward sloping, and vertical. Each segment corresponds to a different set of economic circumstances. For example, the horizontal segment corresponds to relatively low levels of GDP where unemployment is high and resources are readily available. Output can increase without putting any pressure on the price level. The upward-sloping segment shows that at these higher GDP levels the once readily available resources are becoming less readily available. To hire more resources, firms raise resource prices which are passed off in the form of higher prices for the goods and services the resources produce. That is to say, the price level increases. Alternatively, an increase in the price level will increase firms' profits and the response will be an increase in output. The vertical segment corresponds to full employment in the economy. It is impossible to increase real GDP beyond the full employment real GDP level. Only the price level can rise.

The aggregate demand curve is downward sloping for three reasons. First, as the price level decreases, people's real wealth (assets they hold) increases, making them feel relatively more secure to increase their aggregate spending. Second, if lower interest rates are part of the lower price level, then the cost associated with borrowing falls (interest rates on investment projects, mortgage rates on houses, credit payments on cars, and all those many items bought with your credit card) making them less expensive so aggregate spending on consumption and investment increases. Finally, a lower price level will make our goods more attractive to foreigners. Exports, part of our aggregate demand, increase.

The intersection of the aggregate demand curve and aggregate supply curve determines the equilibrium price level and level of real GDP. Shifts can occur in both the aggregate demand and the aggregate supply curves which will shift the equilibrium level's price and real GDP. The aggregate demand curve shifts to the right when there is an increase in the quantity of goods and services demanded at a specific price level. Such a shift might result from an increase in spending on the part of government, consumers, business firms, or foreigners. The aggregate supply curve shifts to the right when resources become more available, such as more workers in the labor force, more capital, or more land.

The aggregate demand and aggregate supply model can be used to describe changes in our real world. For example, the Great Depression that created massive unemployment in the United States and other countries in the 1930s reflects a relatively weak (positioned to the left) aggregate demand curve. World War II, with its incredible demands for war goods production, shifted aggregate demand to the right, causing real GDP to increase. While aggregate demand was shifting the economy toward full employment, the aggregate supply curve was shifting to the left as labor left the private sector for the military. The increase in aggregate demand along with the decrease in aggregate supply caused the price level to rise. The Vietnam era was another war period marked by rising price levels and rising real GDP. Inflation, arising mostly from the demand side, is referred to as *demand-pull inflation*. The OPEC oil embargo of 1973–74 shifted the aggregate supply curve to the left causing an increase in the price level and a decrease in the level of real GDP. This combination is called *stagflation*. Inflation arising from a decrease in aggregate supply is called *cost-push inflation* since higher costs (oil prices, for example) raised the price level. The 1990s witnessed another milder recession stemming from diminished aggregate demand. High levels of consumer spending during the 1980s decreased as credit was restricted in the late 1980s and early 1990s. Many firms that had incurred large debts during the 1980s had to reduce their employment in the early 1990s due to the reduction in consumer spending.

Government policies can be developed to cope with some of the problems associated with adverse shifts in the aggregate demand and aggregate supply curves. However, creating and implementing these policies are enormously complicated in a real-world setting. Above all, a clear understanding of the nature of the problems of high unemployment and high inflation is essential to developing policies to combat them. The aggregate demand and aggregate supply model is a tool that will help us to better understand these problems.

Key Terms — Test your comprehension by defining and explaining the significance of each of these terms.

recession
depression
prosperity
inflation
business cycle
trough
recovery
peak
downturn
gross domestic product
price indexes
nominal GDP

real GDP
consumer price index
base year
price level
GDP deflator
aggregate supply
aggregate demand
macroequilibrium
demand-pull inflation
stagflation
cost-push inflation
leveraged buyout

True-False Questions — If a statement is false, explain why.

1. Aggregate demand is basically the same concept as demand for a good or service, such as a banana or health services that are the subject of analysis in microeconomics. (T/F)

2. One reason why the aggregate demand curve is downward sloping is because as the price level decreases, real wealth increases so that people save less and consume more. (T/F)

3. The vertical segment of the aggregate supply curve suggests that ample resources are available to increase real GDP. (T/F)

4. The most general measure of inflation is the consumer price index. (T/F)

5. The focus of microeconomic analysis is on individual behavior while macroeconomics focuses on the behavior of the national economy. (T/F)

6. If an increase in the price level creates higher profits and, as a result, causes real GDP to increase, then the aggregate supply curve must be vertical. (T/F)

7. The Great Depression was a period in American economic history marked by significant cost-push inflation. (T/F)

8. Real GDP remains constant if increases in the price level alone cause nominal GDP to increase. (T/F)

9. In order for a recession to exist, a decline in the nation's GDP must persist for at least half a year. (T/F)

10. If the trend line drawn through an economy's business cycle is very steep then we conclude that the economy's annual rate of growth over the cycle is sluggish, that is, relatively low. (T/F)

11. The usefulness of CPI diminishes as the prices measured become more distant from the base year. (T/F)

12. The upward-sloping portion of the aggregate supply curve suggests that an increase in the price level will be associated with an increase in real GDP. (T/F)

13. A cut in government spending will cause the aggregate demand curve to shift to the right. (T/F)

14. When the value of goods and services demanded in the economy is equal to the value of goods and services produced, the economy is in macroequilibrium. (T/F)

15. The price increase associated with increased aggregate demand during World War II was exacerbated by a decrease in aggregate supply caused by a labor force shift to the military. (T/F)

16. Demand-pull inflation occurs when increases in aggregate demand shift the aggregate demand curve to the right while the aggregate supply curve remains unchanged at full employment real GDP. (T/F)

17. Stagflation occurs when levels of unemployment and inflation are low. (T/F)

18. Leveraged buyouts in the 1980s caused firms to cut back on employment in order to meet their debt payments in the face of lower consumer demand. (T/F)

19. At any time, a market economy tends toward full employment and zero inflation. (T/F)

20. An increase in government spending should decrease unemployment when the economy's in recession. (T/F)

Multiple Choice Questions

1. The upward slope of the trend line through a business cycle indicates that
   a. the economy is in a recovery phase.
   b. the economy is in a period of stagflation.
   c. there is a positive relationship between real GDP and the price level.
   d. the economy's output increases.
   e. the quantity supplied of a certain good increases as the price decreases.

2. One characteristic of the recovery phase of the business cycle is that
   a. upward pressure on the economy's price level begins to build.
   b. output reaches its maximum level.
   c. a recession will soon follow.
   d. inflation is moderating.
   e. unemployment is increasing.

3. One way that the government can increase aggregate demand is by
   a. reducing government spending.
   b. reducing income taxes.
   c. increasing corporate income taxes.
   d. creating stagflation.
   e. reducing the economy's supply of labor.

4. The measure that compares the prices of all goods and services produced in the economy in any year to the prices of those goods and services produced in a base year is known as
   a. the GDP deflator.
   b. the real GDP.
   c. the nominal GDP.
   d. the CPI.
   e. the PPI.

5. All of the following conditions are consistent with general prosperity in the economy except
   a. unemployment is relatively low.
   b. wage rates are relatively high.
   c. real GDP is relatively high.
   d. morale among workers and management is relatively high.
   e. the price level decreases.

6. It is important to control for price increases when comparing GDP between two years because
   a. nominal GDP can rise due either to an increase in output or an increase in the price level.
   b. economists are only interested in price changes.
   c. price increases are usually larger in relative terms than quantity increases.
   d. price increases can reduce nominal GDP.
   e. price increases can increase real GDP.

7. The GDP deflator
   a. measures changes in the cost of a fixed basket of consumer goods and services.
   b. measures the severity of a recession.
   c. measures the ratio of a fixed basket of investment goods to a fixed basket of consumer goods.
   d. is used to calculate nominal GDP.
   e. is the price index generally used to calculate real GDP from nominal GDP data.

8. The vertical segment of the aggregate supply curve
   a. represents high unemployment nominal GDP.
   b. represents full employment real GDP.
   c. is called the Keynesian segment of the aggregate supply curve.
   d. is called the intermediate segment of the aggregate supply curve.
   e. suggests that idle resources are plentiful in the economy.

9. The aggregate supply curve shifts to the right when
   a. supplies of resources increase.
   b. wage rates increase.
   c. consumption decreases.
   d. investment increases.
   e. population decreases.

10. The CPI
    a. measures changes in the cost of a fixed basket of consumer goods and services.
    b. measures the severity of a recession.
    c. measures the ratio of a fixed basket of investment goods to a fixed basket of consumer goods.
    d. is used to calculate nominal GDP.
    e. is the price index generally used to calculate real GDP from nominal GDP data.

11. The difference between nominal and real GDP is that
    a. nominal GDP includes price changes while real GDP doesn't.
    b. nominal GDP measures aggregate supply while real GDP measures aggregate demand.
    c. real GDP is always equal to or higher than nominal GDP, depending on the phase of the business cycle.
    d. real GDP includes price changes while nominal GDP doesn't.
    e. real GDP is derived from the CPI while nominal GDP is derived from the GDP deflator.

12. In the aggregate demand and aggregate supply model, the intersection of the AD and AS curves determines
    a. the price level and real GDP.
    b. the level of employment.
    c. the difference between real and nominal GDP.
    d. the price level and the rate of inflation.
    e. the rate of economic growth.

13. The sequence of phases in a business cycle is
    a. recovery, recession, prosperity, downturn.
    b. prosperity, recovery, downturn, recession.
    c. prosperity, downturn, recovery, recession.
    d. recession, recovery, prosperity, downturn.
    e. recession, recovery, downturn, prosperity.

14. The aggregate supply curve shifts to the right when
    a. consumers, with no change in nominal GDP, save less and consume more.
    b. consumers, with no change in nominal GDP, save more and consume less.
    c. people, with no change in the price level, decrease their supply of labor.
    d. people, with no change in the price level, increase their supply of labor.
    e. as a result of war, people shift from civilian to military production.

15. If nominal GDP is $2,000 billion and the GDP deflator is 125, then real GDP is
    a. $1,600 billion.
    b. $2,500 billion.
    c. $1,800 billion.
    d. $2,400 billion.
    e. $1,000 billion.

16. If the price level in the United States increases while price levels elsewhere remain unchanged
    a. aggregate supply in the U.S. shifts to the right.
    b. aggregate demand in other economies shifts to the left.
    c. real GDP in the U.S. increases more rapidly than in other economies.
    d. U.S. exports increase, shifting U.S. aggregate demand to the right.
    e. U.S. exports decrease, shifting U.S. aggregate demand to the left.

17. The aggregate demand curve shifts to the right when
    a. consumers, with no change in real GDP, save less and consume more.
    b. consumers, with no change in real GDP, save more and consume less.
    c. people, with no change in the price level, decrease their supply of labor.
    d. people, with no change in the price level, increase their supply of labor.
    e. as a result of war, people shift from civilian to military production.

18. If more capital is made available in an economy, one consequence would be
    a. a decrease in aggregate demand.
    b. an increase in aggregate demand.
    c. greater unemployment.
    d. a shift to the right in the aggregate supply curve.
    e. an increase in the slope of the upward-sloping portion of the aggregate supply curve.

19. Cost-push inflation is the type of inflation associated with
    a. the OPEC reduction in the supply of oil in 1973.
    b. military spending during a war.
    c. the Great Society programs.
    d. the New Deal era.
    e. the stock market crash in 1929.

20. One of the options for government to reduce the level of unemployment is to
    a. increase taxes.
    b. increase government spending.
    c. limit imports.
    d. reduce the money supply.
    e. shift the aggregate supply curve to the right.

Problems

1. Suppose the GDP deflator is 140 for 1993. The base year is 1990. If nominal GDP in 1993 is 3.6 trillion dollars, calculate its real GDP. Show your work.

2. Suppose that the cost of the market basket of goods and services that represents the CPI is $3000 in the base year, 1987. Suppose also that the cost of the same market basket of goods in 1989 was $3300. What was the value of the CPI index for 1989? Explain what 1989 CPI means.

3. Suppose the value of the same market basket as in question 3 was $4000 in 1991. What was the average annual rate of inflation between 1989 and 1991? Show your work.

4. Use an aggregate demand/aggregate supply diagram to show what happened to the economy as a result of the OPEC oil embargo in 1973.

Discussion Questions

1. Define gross domestic product. How can GDP increase over time?

2. How is the consumer price index constructed?

3. Why do we say that the GDP deflator is a broader measure of inflation than the consumer price index?

4. What's the difference between nominal GDP and real GDP?

5. Why is the aggregate supply curve in three distinct segments?

6. Why is the aggregate demand curve downward sloping?

7. Distinguish between demand-pull inflation and cost-push inflation.

Answers to Questions

True-False Questions

1. False because aggregate demand refers to all goods and services purchased in the economy while demand refers to the goods or services purchased in one market.
2. True
3. False because the vertical segment indicates full employment.
4. False because the most general measure is the GDP deflator.
5. True
6. False because aggregate supply must be upward sloping for output to increase as the price level increases.
7. False because the Great Depression suggested high unemployment and stable or falling prices.
8. True
9. True
10. False because a steep trend line indicates rapid growth.
11. True
12. True
13. False because an increase in government spending increases aggregate demand.
14. True
15. True
16. True
17. False because stagflation occurs when unemployment and inflation are high.
18. True
19. False because market economies can show either high unemployment or high inflation.
20. True

Multiple Choice Questions

1. d	6. a	11. a	16. e
2. a	7. e	12. a	17. a
3. b	8. b	13. d	18. d
4. a	9. a	14. d	19. a
5. e	10. a	15. a	20. b

Problems

1. Real GDP is equal to nominal GDP divided by the GDP deflator expressed as a decimal or, in this case, $3.6 trillion/1.4 which is $2.57 trillion.

2. The value of the CPI is 3300/3000 multiplied by 100 which is 110. The inflation rate between 1987 and 1989 was 10 percent.

3. The value of the CPI for 1991 is 4000/3300 multiplied by 100 which is 133. The average annual rate of inflation between 1989 and 1991 is 133 − 110/110 multiplied by 100 then divided by 2 or 10.45 percent.

4. Your graph should look like the one shown here. The OPEC embargo was a supply shock raising the price of oil. Due to an extreme increase in the price of an essential input, the price level generally rose. The aggregate supply curve shifted to the left. These events are shown in the following diagram by a shift in the aggregate supply curve from AS to AS', a decrease in the equilibrium level of GDP to GDP', and a rise in the equilibrium price level to P'.

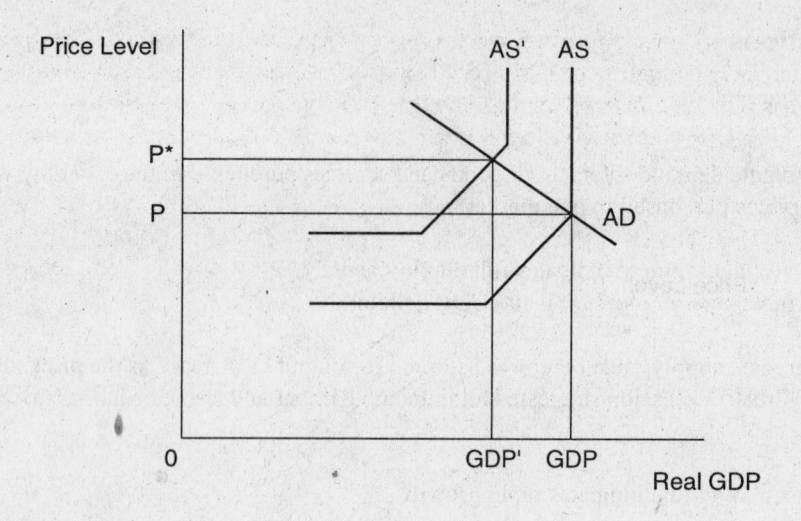

Discussion Questions

1. Gross domestic product is the total value of all final goods and services produced in a country during a calendar year. GDP can increase if the quantity of goods and services produced increases or if the price of these goods and services increases.

2. The consumer price index is constructed by dividing the cost of a fixed market basket of goods and services purchased in a particular year by the cost of the same market basket of goods and services in a base year and multiplying by 100. The market basket represents purchases made by the typical American household.

3. The GDP deflator includes the prices of all final goods and services produced in a year while the CPI includes only purchases of consumer goods and services.

4. Nominal GDP, measured in current dollars, includes the effect of price changes. Real GDP, measured in constant dollars, excludes price changes.

5. Each segment of the aggregate supply curve reflects a different set of macroeconomic circumstances. For example, the horizontal segment reflects an economy operating well below full employment so that real GDP can be increased without any upward pressure on the price level. The upward-sloping segment shows that resources are becoming more scarce as the economy approaches full employment. Employers bid for resources, driving up their prices, which causes costs of production and the price level to rise. Alternatively, price level increases raise employers' profits so they increase output. In the vertical segment, full employment exists and resources are unavailable to increase real GDP. Only the price level can rise.

6. The aggregate demand curve is downward sloping because of the real wealth effect, the interest rate effect, and the international trade effect. As the price level decreases, the purchasing power of wealth increases. As the price level decreases, investment spending and consumer spending increase because interest rates decrease. As the price level decreases, foreign demand for exports increases.

CHAPTER 4 AGGREGATE DEMAND AND AGGREGATE SUPPLY

7. Demand-pull inflation arises from a rightward shift in the aggregate demand function. Cost-push inflation arises from a leftward shift in the aggregate supply function. Demand-pull inflation is shown in the following figure. A rightward shift in the aggregate demand curve when the economy is at full employment causes the price level to increase from P to P'. The OPEC embargo is an example of an event that caused cost-push inflation. The figure for this is shown in the answer to problem 4.

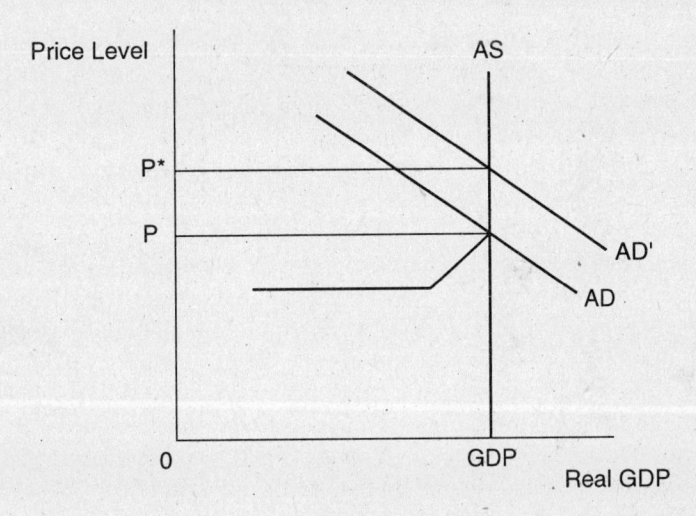

CHAPTER 5

GROSS DOMESTIC PRODUCT ACCOUNTING

Chapter Summary

The circular flow model explains why the value of resources used to produce goods and services in an economy is equal to the value of the goods and services produced. Money is the fluid that makes it all work. It is used to pay households for the resources that they supply to producers. Households pay producers for the goods and services they consume. One dollar in income to a resource supplier shows up as a dollar's worth of output in the product market. The circular flow of money, resources, goods and services summarizes the two approaches to GDP accounting—the expenditure approach and the income approach.

The expenditure approach—what people (in our economy and elsewhere), businesses, and government spend on goods and services—includes four categories: personal consumption, gross private domestic investment, government purchases, and net exports (the difference between exports and imports). Only final goods and services are counted to avoid double counting. Personal consumption expenditures include spending on durable goods, nondurable goods, and services. Gross private domestic investment includes spending on new factories, tools, and machinery as well as spending to replace worn-out plants and equipment, spending on residential structures, and changes in business inventories. Government purchases a range of goods and services from defense-related items to the postal service. Most government spending is done by state and local governments. Net exports represent the difference between a country's exports and imports.

The income approach focuses on the sum of the payments made to resource owners who produce the goods and services bought by the people, businesses and government. These income payments include compensation to employees, interest, corporate profit, rental income, and proprietors' income. The sum of these incomes is called national income. Compensation to employees is by far the largest of these categories. Interest is paid to savers for the use of their funds. Corporate profit is divided between dividends that go to shareholders, profit that is reinvested in the corporation, and corporate profit tax paid to the government. Proprietors' income is paid to the owners of unincorporated businesses.

Note the distinction between gross domestic product (GDP) and gross national product (GNP). The difference is ownership and location. GDP measures location—what is produced and earned in the domestic economy. GNP measures ownership—what the nation's people (wherever they are) produce and earn. Net domestic product (NDP) is GDP minus capital depreciation, and national income is GDP minus indirect taxes. If there were no taxes or depreciation, GDP would equal national income. Two other income measures are also useful to economists. These are personal income, the amount that households actually receive as income, and disposable personal income, personal income minus direct taxes. Disposable personal income is either spent or saved by households.

GDP is a good approximation, but not a full accounting, of overall economic activity in an economy. It fails to include the value of housework (isn't that useful, productive work?), activity of the underground economy, leisure, and improvements in the quality of goods and services. The cost of environmental damage should be netted out of GDP, but isn't. In spite of these exclusions, GDP is still a solid measure of the economy's level of performance.

CHAPTER 5 GROSS DOMESTIC PRODUCT ACCOUNTING

Key Terms — Test your comprehension by identifying and explaining the significance of these terms.

circular flow of goods, services, and resources
circular flow of money
final goods
intermediate goods
value added
personal consumption expenditures
gross private domestic investment
expenditure approach
government purchases
net exports
durable goods
nondurable goods

services
inventory investment
income approach
national income
gross national product (GNP)
capital depreciation
net domestic product (NDP)
personal income
transfer payments
disposable personal income
underground economy

True-False Questions — If a statement is false, explain why.

1. The circular flow model shows equivalent streams of resources for production, final goods and services, and money to pay for the resources and the final goods and services. (T/F)

2. Consumption spending forms a relatively small share of total output. (T/F)

3. A final good or service is produced for resale. (T/F)

4. Sales of second-hand cars would be included in GDP. (T/F)

5. Gross private domestic investment includes government spending on the national guard but excludes other military spending. (T/F)

6. An increase in net exports causes GDP to decrease. (T/F)

7. GDP would increase if the value of underground economy transactions was included. (T/F)

8. Disposable income is equal to personal income plus transfer payments. (T/F)

9. Durable goods are expected to last at least five years. (T/F)

10. Among the goods and services that the government purchases are transportation facilities. (T/F)

11. The proportion of GDP in the categories consumption, investment, government spending and net exports is quite different in the United States compared to other industrialized countries. (T/F)

12. National income measures the sum of all payments made to resource owners for the use of their resources. (T/F)

13. Interest is a payment to people who make profits in their businesses. (T/F)

14. Shareholders in corporations receive proprietor's income. (T/F)

15. GDP and GNP are precisely equal to each other. (T/F)

16. Personal income minus personal taxes is equal to disposable income. (T/F)

17. If people in a household hire a housekeeper rather than keep house themselves, they increase GDP. (T/F)

18. Environmental damage actually adds to GDP because resources must be devoted to cleaning up after environmental damage. (T/F)

19. As a percentage of GDP, the underground economy is probably bigger in Europe than in the United States. (T/F)

20. Because GDP isn't a perfect representation of production in the economy, it isn't that useful to economists. (T/F)

Multiple Choice Questions

1. The difference between GDP and GNP is that
   a. factor payments to foreign-owned firms in the United States are included in GNP.
   b. depreciation is excluded from GNP.
   c. the corporate profits tax is excluded from GDP.
   d. indirect business taxes are counted twice in GDP.
   e. factor payments to foreign-owned firms in the United States are included in GDP.

2. The circular flow model of GDP shows the interdependence of
   a. the supplies of goods and the supplies of services.
   b. firms and investment.
   c. intermediate goods and final goods.
   d. net imports and net exports.
   e. money for goods and services and money for resources.

3. The smallest portion of personal consumption expenditures is accounted for by
   a. inventory investment.
   b. productivity.
   c. purchases of services.
   d. purchases of nondurable goods.
   e. purchases of durable goods.

4. The expenditure approach to GDP accounting is the sum of expenditures in all of the following categories except
   a. gross private domestic investment.
   b. consumption spending.
   c. government spending on goods and services.
   d. transfer payments by the government.
   e. the difference between exports and imports.

5. The income approach to GDP accounting differs from the expenditure approach in that
   a. the income approach computes total payments made to households that provide the resources used to produce final goods and services.
   b. the income approach excludes transfer payments but the expenditure approach doesn't.
   c. the income approach subtracts the net exports of goods and services.
   d. the income approach can only be calculated for middle and upper income households.
   e. the income approach only computes total income from those households with two wage earners.

6. If a large number of Egypt's citizens work overseas, then perhaps the best measure of the Egyptian people's economic health is
   a. the GDP deflator.
   b. real GNP.
   c. real GDP.
   d. nominal GNP.
   e. nominal GDP.

7. The income approach calculates GDP with all of the following except
   a. interest.
   b. wages.
   c. rent.
   d. investment.
   e. profits.

8. A decline in inventories shows up as
   a. a decrease in gross private domestic investment.
   b. increases in production.
   c. an increase in gross private domestic investment.
   d. a decrease in production.
   e. decreases in services.

9. Disposable income is
   a. taxes and transfer payments.
   b. a household's consumption expenditures.
   c. a household's savings.
   d. expenditures on luxury items by households.
   e. the sum of consumption and saving.

10. The circular flow model
    a. is also called the Keynesian model.
    b. represents the relationship between households and government.
    c. includes both the expenditures approach and the income approach.
    d. shows inequality between income and expenditures.
    e. suggests that economics is biological.

11. In the circular flow model, a value equivalence exists between
    a. expenditures for goods and services and payments to factors of production.
    b. payments to factors of production and subsidies from the government.
    c. expenditures by government and tax receipts.
    d. GDP and GNP.
    e. GNP and NNP.

12. The expenditures approach calculates
    a. GNP.
    b. payments to resource owners and resources.
    c. national income.
    d. purchases of goods and services.
    e. NNP.

13. If investment is insufficient to cover depreciation, then
    a. GDP is the same as NNP.
    b. GDP will shrink over time.
    c. gross investment exceeds depreciation.
    d. inventory investment is positive.
    e. capital stock grows.

14. It is necessary to subtract _____ from net domestic product in order to compute national income.
    a. indirect business taxes
    b. capital depreciation
    c. transfer payments
    d. net exports
    e. factor payments to the rest of the world

15. The largest share of national income is accounted for by
    a. corporate profit.
    b. proprietors' income.
    c. compensation of employees.
    d. consumption of nondurable goods.
    e. income taxes.

16. GDP minus capital depreciation is
    a. GNP.
    b. net private domestic investment.
    c. net domestic product (NDP).
    d. a transfer payment.
    e. the CPI.

17. All of the following are categories of investment except
    a. gross private domestic investment.
    b. inventory investment.
    c. investment in new capital equipment.
    d. investment in residential housing.
    e. investment in mutual funds.

18. The largest component in consumption expenditures is
    a. compensation to employees.
    b. profits.
    c. rents and royalties.
    d. services.
    e. proprietors' income.

19. The value-added approach to GDP computation involves
    a. problems with double counting.
    b. subtracting income from expenditures.
    c. summing the addition to value at each stage in production.
    d. summing the price times quantity for all intermediate goods.
    e. improving technology so that value is added at each stage.

20. One of the reasons for not including such items as leisure in the calculation of GDP is that
    a. including these items is conceptually difficult.
    b. these are not government sanctioned items.
    c. these items are not valued on the market and therefore are difficult to estimate.
    d. to include these items would cause GDP to decrease.
    e. these are not productive items.

Problems

1. Determine the value added in the following case.

Firm	Good	Market value	Value added by firm
bauxite mining	bauxite	$10	
aluminum sheeting	aluminum	$22	
kitchen sink	kitchen sink	$40	

2. Using the following data, derive GDP, NDP, national income, personal income, and personal disposal income.

personal consumption expenditures	$490	indirect business taxes	70
interest	40	imports	30
corporate profit	70	proprietors' income	55
government purchases	150	income tax	100
depreciation	40	income earned but not received	60
rent	20	income received but not earned	70
gross private domestic investment	50	factor incomes to overseas	25
compensation of employees	420	exports	50
factor incomes from overseas	30		

Discussion Questions

1. How do the two approaches to GDP accounting relate to the circular flow model?

2. Approximately what percent of GDP is represented in each of the four expenditures categories?

3. Why are inventories counted as part of investment?

4. Approximately what percent of national income is represented in each of its categories?

5. Why would an economist, interested in a country's rate of growth, look at its NDP rather than GDP?

6. If you were studying living standards in a country, which measure would you find more informative, national income or personal income? Why?

7. How could increases in leisure over time be included in the calculation of GDP?

Answers to Questions

True-False Questions

1. True
2. False because consumption spending can account for over 70 percent of GDP.
3. False because a final good or service goes to its ultimate user or consumer.
4. False because a used car has already been counted as part of a previous year's GDP.
5. False because government spending is separate from gross private domestic investment.
6. False because an increase in net exports causes GDP to increase.
7. True
8. False because disposable personal income is equal to personal income minus direct taxes.
9. False because durable goods last for at least one year.
10. True
11. False because among industrialized countries these proportions are about the same.
12. True
13. False because interest is paid to people who lend money.
14. False because shareholders receive dividends as income.
15. False because GNP is equal to GDP plus factor payments to Americans producing overseas minus factor payments to foreigners producing in the United States.
16. True
17. True
18. True
19. True
20. False because GDP still gives a good indication of recessions and expansions in the economy.

Multiple Choice Questions

1. e	6. b	11. a	16. c
2. e	7. d	12. d	17. e
3. e	8. a	13. b	18. d
4. d	9. e	14. a	19. c
5. a	10. c	15. c	20. c

Problems

1. bauxite mining $10
   aluminum sheeting $12
   kitchen sink $18

2. GDP = $710   national income = $605
   GDP = $670   personal income = $615
                        personal disposable income = $515

Discussion Questions

1. The expenditure approach corresponds to the money flow from households, businesses, government, and the international sector purchasing final goods and services. The income approach corresponds to the money flow from buyers of resources to the households that supply those resources for use in production. The two money flows should be equivalent.

2. Consumption is by far the largest category of expenditure. Consumption accounted for some 68 percent of GDP in 1993. Government spending accounted for approximately 18 percent of 1993 GDP, investment accounted for another 14 percent, and net exports were negative. As a percentage of GDP, the difference between exports and imports was about 1 percent.

3. Inventories are counted as part of investment because firms must maintain stocks of inputs and stocks of finished goods in order to produce and sell.

4. Compensation of employees dwarfs all the other categories at about 74 percent of the total in 1993. Rental income was only .5 percent of the total in 1993. Corporate profit, net interest, and proprietors' income were 9.5 percent, 7.8 percent, and 8.6 percent of national income, respectively, in 1993.

5. NDP is perhaps of greater interest because it excludes investment expenditures to replace used-up capital. NDP focuses on investment net of depreciation. An economy must have positive net investment in order to grow over time.

6. Personal income is probably more useful. This is because personal income shows the income that people actually receive, including transfer payments. Also, certain taxes that are withheld from income, like social security taxes, are accounted for by personal income. Personal income minus direct taxes gives disposable personal income.

7. Leisure could be valued at the wage rate for which someone might have worked had they not been enjoying leisure. However, there are problems encountered in doing this calculation. For example, perhaps working more hours wasn't an option. To a large extent, the length of the working day is institutionally determined. This is especially true in Europe where workers are sometimes required by law to take vacations!

CHAPTER 6

BUILDING THE KEYNESIAN MODEL: CONSUMPTION AND INVESTMENT

Chapter Summary

What people decide to spend and save and what producers decide to produce for consumption and for investment are decisions they make simultaneously and independently of each other. Because of this independence, there can be no guarantee that all the consumption goods produced will actually be bought. This lack of symmetry between consumption-spending decisions and consumption-production decisions explains, at least for some economists, why GDP may be rising or falling. For this reason, we want to study people's behavior with respect to consumption, saving, and investment.

A number of models explaining why people consume what they do have been developed. John Maynard Keynes' absolute income hypothesis asserts that consumption is a function of income. The character of that relationship is this: Consumption increases as income increases, but at a diminishing rate. To illustrate, if Brenda's income increases from $10,000 to $11,000, she will increase her consumption spending by $900. If her income increases from $11,000 to $12,000, her consumption spending will increase by $800. What is true for Brenda is true as well for the national economy. National consumption is a function of national income and it increases by smaller amounts as national income increases. Keynes defines the *marginal propensity to consume* as the change in consumption divided by the change in income.

Although Keynes believed that the marginal propensity to consume decreases as income increases, Simon Kuznets' empirical research showed that the marginal propensity to consume is actually constant. James Duesenberry explained why. According to him, consumption is rooted in status. If everyone's income doubled, everyone's relative income position would remain the same. It's their relative position that determines their marginal propensity to consume.

Milton Friedman's permanent income hypothesis differentiates between permanent and transitory income. The marginal propensity to consume, he argues, relates consumption to permanent income. Changes in transitory income change saving. Franco Modigliani based his theory of consumption on a person's behavior over their life-cycle. Young people's marginal propensity to consume is high. Their incomes are still relatively low, but they are raising families. In their middle years, their marginal propensity to consume falls because their income rises faster than their consumption. In their retiring years, marginal propensity to consume rises because their incomes fall faster than their consumption. If the population's age distribution remains relatively constant, then the marginal propensity to consume will be relatively constant.

The marginal propensity to consume appears as a straight-line curve—consumption measured on the vertical, income on the horizontal axis—originating some distance above the horizontal because of *autonomous consumption,* which is greater than zero when income is zero. The consumption curve shifts with changes in real asset and money holdings, expectations of price changes, credit and interest rate changes, and tax changes. We write a consumption equation—$C = a + bY$—where a is autonomous consumption, b is the marginal propensity to consume, and Y is the level of national income.

National income is either spent or saved, $Y = C + S,$ where S is equal to saving. Rearranging the equation and substituting the consumption equation for $C,$ we derive $S = Y - (a + bY).$ Saving appears in a graph of the consumption curve as the vertical distance between the consumption curve and the income (C + S) or 45° line. At the level of national income where the consumption curve intersects the 45° line, saving is zero. At lower levels of national income, saving is negative (dissaving). At higher levels, saving is positive. *The marginal propensity to save is* $(1 - MPC).$

CHAPTER 6 CONSUMPTION AND INVESTMENT

Intended investment, regarded as autonomous because it is independent of the level of national income, is determined by a variety of factors including the level of technology, the interest rate, expectations of future economic growth, and the rate of capacity utilization. Investment tends to be quite volatile.

As we will see in the next chapter, consumption, saving, and investment interact to determine the economy's equilibrium level of national income.

Key Terms — Test your comprehension by defining and explaining the significance of these terms.

consumption function
absolute income hypothesis
marginal propensity to consume
relative income hypothesis
permanent income hypothesis
life-cycle hypothesis
permanent income

transitory income
autonomous consumption
saving
marginal propensity to save
45-degree line
intended investment
autonomous investment

True-False Questions — If a statement is false, explain why.

1. Consumption-spending decisions are carefully coordinated with consumption-production decisions in our economy. (T/F)

2. The most important factor determining people's consumption behavior is the level of their income. (T/F)

3. Keynes' absolute income hypothesis asserts that as income increases consumption increases, but at a decreasing rate. (T/F)

4. Keynes believed that the marginal propensity to consume is constant. (T/F)

5. Simon Kuznets' data supported the idea that marginal propensity to consume is constant. (T/F)

6. Duesenberry's relative income hypothesis suggests that status explains why the marginal propensity to consume is constant.

7. If everybody's incomes increase at the same rate, then their relative incomes increase as well. (T/F)

8. Modigliani's life-cycle hypothesis suggests that consumption fluctuates less than income over a person's lifetime. (T/F)

9. The expectation that the price level will increase induces consumers to save less and consume more now, which raises (upward shift) the consumption function. (T/F)

10. If autonomous consumption increases, then the consumption curve shifts up. (T/F)

11. An increase in interest rates shifts the consumption curve downward. (T/F)

12. We can determine consumption spending for any income level knowing the level of autonomous consumption and the marginal propensity to consume. (T/F)

13. The saving curve always coincides with the intended investment curve. (T/F)

14. Changes in investment are independent of the absolute level of national income. (T/F)

15. Because intended investment is related to the level of national income, it is called autonomous investment. (T/F)

16. Introduction of new technology causes the level of investment to increase. (T/F)

17. A decrease in the interest rate causes the level of investment to decrease. (T/F)

18. Changes in the rate of capital utilization have little influence on investment. (T/F)

19. Investment is highly volatile. (T/F)

20. When consumption exceeds national income, dissaving occurs. (T/F)

Multiple Choice Questions

1. The following are characteristics of intended investment except
   a. its level is influenced by the rate of capacity utilization.
   b. as the interest rate falls, the quantity of intended investment increases.
   c. its size is dependent on the level of national income.
   d. it is volatile in nature.
   e. its level is influenced by the introduction of new technologies.

2. Milton Friedman proposed the
   a. permanent income hypothesis.
   b. life-cycle hypothesis.
   c. absolute income hypothesis.
   d. relative income hypothesis.
   e. saving equals investment hypothesis.

3. The most important factor(s) determining consumption spending in the Keynesian model is (are)
   a. changes in purchasing power.
   b. the price level.
   c. national income.
   d. aggregate supply.
   e. intended investment plus saving.

4. The life-cycle hypothesis on consumption behavior suggests that people, over the course of a life-cycle,
   a. spend everything they earn so that saving ends up at zero.
   b. increase their marginal propensity to consume as income increases.
   c. decrease their marginal propensity to consume as income increases.
   d. have differing MPCs, which is still consistent with a constant MPC for the economy.
   e. consume according to class status.

5. The following are examples of Friedman's transitory income concept except
   a. a jockey winning the triple crown—Kentucky Derby, the Preakness, and Belmont—in one year.
   b. a $10 million winner of the Texas lottery.
   c. a farmer whose crops are wiped out by a drought.
   d. a physician treating a 20-fold increase in her patient load during a year-long epidemic.
   e. David Letterman's $14 million salary at CBS.

6. The marginal propensity to save (MPS)
   a. plus MPC = national income.
   b. plus MPC = one.
   c. plus intended investment = one.
   d. minus national income = consumption.
   e. represents the economy's level of savings.

7. In graphing the Keynesian model, the 45° line
   a. represents the intersects for all levels of consumption.
   b. represents the level of intended investment that would equate actual saving.
   c. represents national income curve, or consumption spending plus saving.
   d. cuts the diagonal at the point where consumption equals savings.
   e. cuts the diagonal at the point where saving equals intended investment.

8. Because intended investment is independent of the level of national income, we graph the investment curve as
   a. downward sloping.
   b. upward sloping.
   c. horizontal.
   d. vertical.
   e. diagonal

9. The change in consumption divided by the change in income is
   a. Keynes' relative income hypothesis.
   b. the marginal propensity to consume.
   c. $a = bY_d$.
   d. the average propensity to consume.
   e. autonomous consumption.

10. Keynes' absolute income hypothesis cannot be correct because
    a. as disposable income increases, consumption increases at a diminishing rate.
    b. the marginal propensity to consume is constant.
    c. rich households save a larger fraction of additional income than poor households.
    d. income is never absolute and thus a hypothesis can't be formed.
    e. autonomous consumption doesn't exist.

11. Autonomous consumption refers to
    a. MPCs that are less than one.
    b. MPCs that are greater than one.
    c. consumption that is independent of the level of income.
    d. permanent consumption associated with Friedman's permanent income hypothesisis.
    e. transitory consumption associated with Friedman's permanent income hypothesis.

12. Shifts in the consumption curve are caused by all of the following except
    a. changes in asset holdings.
    b. changes in income.
    c. changes in price level expectations.
    d. changes in credit availability.
    e. changes in interest rates.

13. When the consumption curve is drawn through the origin
    a. consumption and income are the same.
    b. the marginal propensity to consume is zero.
    c. autonomous saving is very high.
    d. autonomous consumption is zero.
    e. the marginal propensity to consume will decrease as income increases.

14. If the government increases taxes
    a. the intended investment curve shifts upward.
    b. the consumption curve shifts upward.
    c. the consumption curve shifts downward.
    d. national income decreases because people's net income after tax has fallen.
    e. the actual investment curve shifts downward.

15. When MPS = 0.30 and autonomous consumption is $30 billion then
    a. MPC = 0.30.
    b. consumption sending = $10 billion.
    c. MPC = 0.70.
    d. consumption spending = $900 billion.
    e. MPC = 1.00.

16. The marginal propensity to consume is
    a. the amount of consumption that an individual spends out of a given income.
    b. autonomous consumption that an individual spends out of a given income.
    c. income divided by consumption.
    d. change in consumption divided by a change in income.
    e. change in income divided by a change in consumption.

17. The demand curve for investment is downward sloping. Graphed, it shows _____ on the horizontal axis and _____ on the vertical axis.
    a. income, investment
    b. investment, income
    c. investment, the interest rate
    d. the interest rate, investment
    e. income, the interest rate

CHAPTER 6 CONSUMPTION AND INVESTMENT

18. All of the following are determinants of autonomous investment except
    a. interest rates.
    b. credit availability.
    c. the level of income.
    d. changes in the level of income.
    e. the pace of technological change.

19. According to Keynes, the nation's marginal propensity to consume
    a. must be greater than any individual's marginal propensity to consume.
    b. must be less than any individual's marginal propensity to consume.
    c. behaves like the marginal propensity to consume for any individual.
    d. must be equal to every individual's marginal propensity to consume.
    e. is more volatile than any individual's marginal propensity to consume.

20. If stock market prices increase dramatically so that those who own stock perceive that their wealth has increased, then, *ceteris paribus*
    a. the consumption function shifts downward to the right because saving increases.
    b. intended investment increases because it is now more profitable.
    c. the saving curve shifts upward to the left.
    d. the saving curve shifts downward to the right.
    e. the consumption function shifts upward to the left.

Problems

1. a. Suppose that autonomous consumption is $600 and the marginal propensity to consume is 0.60. Write an equation for the consumption curve.

   b. Now write an equation for the saving curve. How are the consumption curve and the saving curve related?

   c. Sketch a graph to show both the consumption curve and the saving curve. Compute the income level at which saving is zero and show this on your graph.

Discussion Questions

1. Why does it make sense to argue that income is the most important determinant of consumption?

2. Suppose that your boss gives you a year-end bonus and you count it as transitory income. Suppose that this happens three years in a row. Would you continue to count this income as transitory? Why or why not?

3. Contrast Keynes' absolute income hypothesis on consumption with Duesenberry's relative income hypothesis. Why was Keynes wrong about the shape of the consumption function?

4. How does an upward shift in the consumption function affect the positioning of the saving function? Graph the effect.

5. Draw a graph that shows the consumption curve, autonomous investment, and the 45° line. Now plot the curve represented by the sum of consumption and autonomous investment at each level of income. What is the position of this curve compared to the consumption curve? Explain.

Answers to Questions

True-False Questions

1. False because consumption-spending and consumption-production decisions are made independently of each other.
2. True
3. True
4. False because he believed the marginal propensity to consume decreases as income increases in Keynes' model.
5. True
6. True
7. False because if all incomes go up at the same rate, relative income is unchanged.
8. True
9. True
10. True
11. True
12. True
13. False because consumers do the saving and producers do the investing so they need not equal.
14. True
15. False because investment is called autonomous since it is unrelated to the level of income.
16. True
17. False because it will cause investment to increase.
18. False because the plant capacity utilization rate is one of the determinants of investment.
19. True
20. True

Multiple Choice Questions

1. c	6. b	11. c	16. d
2. a	7. c	12. b	17. c
3. c	8. c	13. d	18. c
4. d	9. b	14. c	19. c
5. e	10. b	15. c	20. e

Problem

1. a. C = $600 + 0.60Y

   b. S = Y − ($600 + .6Y) or rearranging we have
      S = −$600 + .4Y

   c. A graph with both the consumption and the saving functions follows.

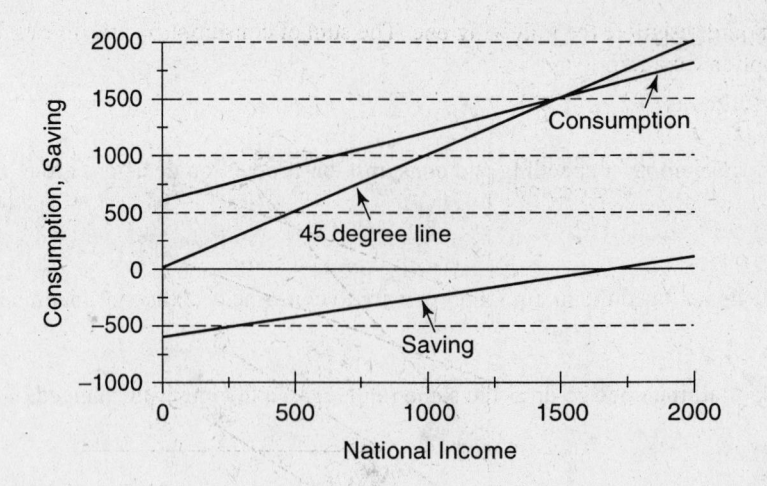

Discussion Questions

1. We can't keep consuming if we have no income. Simple as all that! Consider other determinants—wealth for example. Most people aren't wealthy enough to support their consumption over extended periods entirely from wealth.

2. Probably not. Once income that is initially perceived to be transitory is received in consecutive years it becomes part of permanent income. Is three year's enough? Would you expect to earn bonuses every year? If so, it becomes permanent income.

3. The basic difference between these hypotheses is that Keynes didn't take into consideration the issue of status which Duesenberry did. Keynes was wrong to believe that the marginal propensity to consume falls as income increases.

4. When the consumption curve shifts upward, the saving curve shifts downward by an equal amount. Look at the following graph. When C shifts to C', S shifts down to S'.

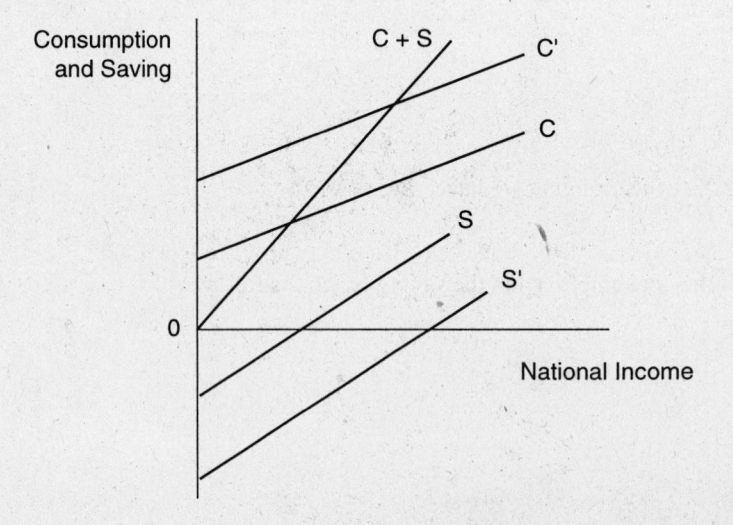

CHAPTER 6 CONSUMPTION AND INVESTMENT

5. Your sketch should resemble the following one. The sum of consumption and investment is drawn exactly parallel to the consumption function.

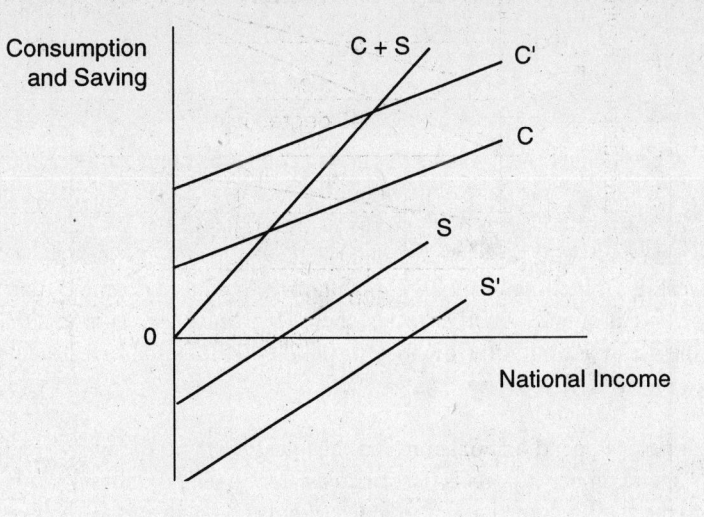

CHAPTER 7

EQUILIBRIUM NATIONAL INCOME IN THE KEYNESIAN MODEL

Chapter Summary

Two very different kinds of people are always at work making decisions concerning spending, saving, and investment that affect each other. The income people earn is spent and saved. Y = C + S. Producers produce an equivalent value of goods and services in the form of consumption and investment. Y = C + I. By definition, C + I = C + S. But the I (investment) in this last equation is actual investment. It's what producers end up investing, not necessarily what they intended to invest, I_i. Sometimes they end up with more actual investment than they intended (creating unwanted inventories) and so cut output. At other times, their actual investment is less than what they intended to produce and, as a result, they increase output. How they respond to their actual investments and why they do it is what this chapter's about.

The total of what people spend on consumption, businesses spend on investment, government spends on its purchases, and foreigners spend on net exports is described as aggregate expenditures. Are these expenditures greater than, less than, or equal to the total income earned in the economy? The answer determines whether national income increases, decreases, or is in equilibrium. In any case, if the economy is not in equilibrium, it is always on its way there. Why is this so?

Suppose the level of national income is $900 billion, autonomous consumption is $60 billion, and the marginal propensity to consume is 0.80. Consumption spending is then $780 billion. C = a + bY. Because Y = $900 billion, if producers, at the same time, intend to invest $100 billion, they end up producing $800 billion of consumption goods. Note: Consumers buy up $780 billion of the $800 billion produced for consumption. As a result, $20 billion of unwanted inventories (which is investment) accumulates. Producers are looking at unsold merchandise. Actual investment is greater than intended investment. What do producers do? Cut output and employment. Fewer people work, so less income is earned. That is to say, national income falls.

Change the numbers slightly. Suppose autonomous consumption and the marginal propensity to consume are the same, but the level of national income is only $700 billion. Consumers now spend $620 billion on consumption. If producers still intend to invest $100 billion, they produce $600 billion for consumption. Now it's not enough. Consumers buy up $20 billion of wanted inventory. Actual investment is less than intended investment. Producers respond by increasing output and employment. More people work, so more income is earned. That is to say, national income increases.

Let's now suppose that national income is $800 billion and intended investment is $100 billion. In this case, consumers spend $700 on consumption, which is exactly what producers produced for consumption. Actual investment equals intended investment. The economy is in equilibrium. The $800 national income is the economy's equilibrium level of national income.

These scenarios can be expressed graphically. The 45°, or income (C + S), line is drawn diagonally from the origin. Because autonomous consumption is greater than zero (it's $60 billion), the aggregate expenditures curve at Y = 0 lies above the income line. And because marginal propensity to consume is less than 1 (it's 0.80), the aggregate expenditures curve is less steep than the income line. They intersect at the equilibrium level of national income. Remember, the aggregate expenditures curve (ignoring government and the foreign sector for now) is equal to C + I. The income curve is equal to C + S. So, at the intersection that represents equilibrium, C + I = C + S.

We can also graph the derivation of the equilibrium level of national income using only the saving and investment curves. The equilibrium level of national income occurs where the saving curve and investment curve intersect. If intended investment is greater than saving, then income rises to bring the two into equality. If saving is greater than intended investment, then national income falls.

Changes in intended investment cause the equilibrium level of national income to change. The relationship between these two changes is explained by the *income multiplier*. Suppose intended investment increases by $100. Suppose Nike decides to invest in another shoe factory. They hire people to build the factory. These people now have $100 added income. They spend $80 on consumption. The people who supplied the $80 of consumption now have $80 added income. They, in turn, use the $80 to buy $64 of consumption goods which becomes other people's added income. These sequential rounds of added income and consumption, all triggered by a one-time $100 increase in Nike's investment, end up creating $500 of new income. This change in national income ($500) caused by a change in investment ($100) defines the income multiplier. The multiplier is equal to 1/1 – MPC. Just as an increase in investment causes a multiple expansion in national income, a decrease in investment will cause a multiple decrease in national income.

The consumers' and producers' behavior that leads the economy to equilibrium also produces a rather surprising consequence known as the *paradox of thrift*. It says: The more people try to save, the more national income will fall, leaving them with no more, and perhaps less, saving in the end. Why? Because an increase in saving is really the same as a decrease in consumption, which is a decrease in aggregate expenditures. It sets in motion a fall in national income to a new and lower level of equilibrium. There, saving is the same or less than it was at the original level of income. Thrift may be personally rewarding but, in this context, it may not be in the best interest of society.

The appendix considers foreign trade as an aggregate expenditure item. Exports add to a country's level of aggregate expenditures. Imports subtract from aggregate expenditures since it represents production located in another country. The aggregate expenditure is either positive or negative, depending on the level of net exports.

Key Terms — Test your comprehension by defining and explaining the significance of the following terms.

aggregate expenditure
equilibrium level of national income
unwanted inventories
actual investment

aggregate expenditure curve (AE)
income multiplier
the paradox of thrift

True-False Questions — If a statement is false, explain why. Questions marked by an asterisk are taken from the chapter appendix.

1. In the Keynesian model, the amount that people intend to save will automatically equal the amount that investors intend to invest. (T/F)

2. Actual investment exceeds intended investment when inventories accumulate. (T/F)

3. If inventories end up being less than intended (or wanted) inventories, then production, employment, and national income will increase. (T/F)

4. Assuming there is no government spending and no foreign trade, then aggregate expenditures in the Keynesian model is given by consumption plus saving. (T/F)

5. For national income to be at equilibrium, consumption spending must be equal to the value of the consumer goods produced. (T/F)

6. When autonomous investment increases by $100, national income will increase by $100. (T/F)

7. A decrease in autonomous investment will have a smaller effect on national income than would an increase in autonomous investment of the same amount. (T/F)

8. The paradox of thrift states that if everyone decided to save more, consumption spending would fall which would decrease national income so that with less income, people would end up saving no more than they did before. (T/F)

9. If the marginal propensity to consume increases, the income multiplier decreases. (T/F)

10. If intended investment is equal to saving, then consumption spending is exactly equal to the value of consumption goods produced in the economy. (T/F)

11. The equality of intended investment and saving leaves open the possibility for inventory reduction. (T/F)

12. When the economy is in equilibrium, intended investment and saving are equal. (T/F)

13. Explaining how the multiplier works: Each new round of spending represents someone else's source of income which, in the succeeding round, becomes the source for a new round of spending. (T/F)

14. The income multiplier is the reciprocal of the marginal propensity to consume. (T/F)

15. The income multiplier is the total change in national income generated by an initial change in autonomous investment. (T/F)

16. The equation for the income multiplier, m, is $m = 1/(1 - MPC)$. (T/F)

17. When the economy's in equilibrium, $C + S = C + I_i$. (T/F)

*18. Imports add to aggregate expenditures; exports subtract from aggregate expenditures. (T/F)

*19. If exports are equal to imports, then foreign trade has no net impact on a country's aggregate expenditures. (T/F)

*20. Restricting imports from other countries, we depress their national incomes and, as a result, adversely affect our own exports to them and, consequently, our own national income. (T/F)

Multiple Choice Questions

1. If actual investment is greater than intended investment, then
   a. the economy is in equilibrium.
   b. national income must rise.
   c. inventory investment is negative.
   d. consumers are purchasing fewer goods and services than are produced.
   e. unemployment will decrease.

2. The simple Keynesian model of national income determination assumes that
   a. aggregate supply is vertical.
   b. aggregate demand increases as the price level decreases.
   c. the price level is constant.
   d. investment is a function of income.
   e. the economy is perfectly competitive.

3. If you read in the paper that intended investment hasn't changed but inventories are accumulating then it is likely that
   a. the economy is about to experience a period of rapid growth.
   b. the price level will rise dramatically.
   c. the economy will experience a drop in production, employment, and income.
   d. the economy will experience a rise in productivity.
   e. intended investment will change.

4. One conclusion that we can draw from a Keynesian analysis of the multiplier effect of autonomous changes in investment is that
   a. recessions associated with downturns in investment are likely to be short lived.
   b. the decrease in national income associated with a decrease in investment will be a multiple of the decrease in investment.
   c. a decrease in investment will be matched by an equal decrease in consumption spending.
   d. intended investment exactly matches savings.
   e. investment increases always lead to multiplier increases in national income that move the economy to full employment.

5. Suppose that the consumption equation is C = $50 + 0.75Y and I = $200. The equilibrium level of national income is
   a. $10,000.
   b. $1,000.
   c. $100.
   d. $750.
   e. $333.33.

6. Using the same information as given in number 5, if the level of national income is actually $1,200, then
   a. inventories will accumulate and production and income will fall.
   b. inventories will accumulate and production and income will rise.
   c. inventories will decline and production and income will rise.
   d. inventories will decline and production and income will fall.
   e. the economy will adjust to a new equilibrium.

7. The graph shows that if the national income level is at $800
   a. inventories will decline and national income will increase.
   b. inventories will decline and national income will decrease.
   c. inventories will increase and national income will decrease.
   d. inventories will increase and national income will increase.
   e. intended investment and savings are equal.

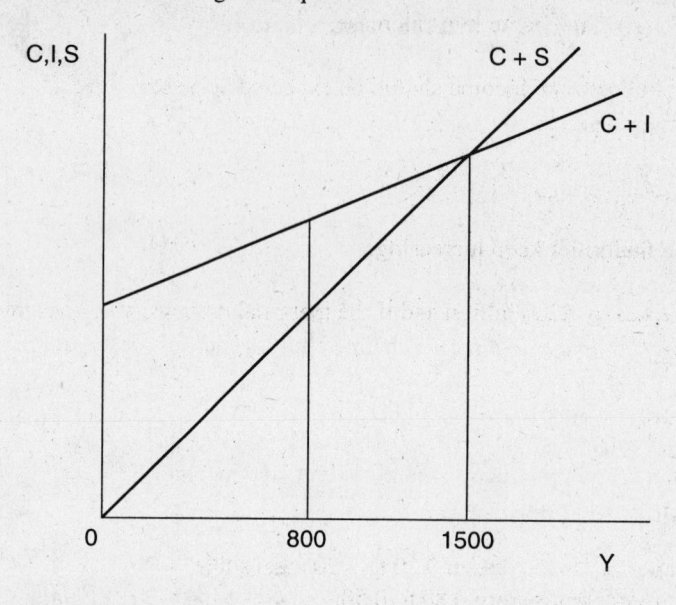

8. According to the operations of the income multiplier, an increase in autonomous investment will
   a. lead to an equal increase in national income.
   b. lead to an increase in national income, which will be a multiple of the increase in investment.
   c. cause the marginal propensity to save to fall.
   d. cause saving to decrease due to the increase in borrowing in the economy.
   e. lead to an equivalent decrease in aggregate expenditures.

9. Given a marginal propensity to consume of 0.90, an increase in investment spending of $100 will lead to a(n)
   a. decrease in national income of $1,000.
   b. increase in national income of $1,000.
   c. increase in national income of $100.
   d. increase in national income of $900.
   e. decrease in national income of $900.

10. The basic idea behind the paradox of thrift is that
    a. by saving more people end up with higher incomes in the future.
    b. it takes money to make money.
    c. an increase in saving decreases national income so much that saving is, at best, unchanged.
    d. it is impossible for savers to increase saving because somebody will always increase spending by an equivalent amount.
    e. saving only benefits producers who invest, not the actual savers.

11. If unwanted inventories caused a decrease in prices instead of national income then we could expect
    a. no increase in unemployment.
    b. savings to rise faster than consumption.
    c. a change in the level of national income equilibrium.
    d. the income multiplier to work in reverse.
    e. intended investment to increase.

12. When consumption goods production is $2,400 billion and consumers purchase $2,000 billion of consumer goods, it is clear that
    a. not enough consumer goods are being produced.
    b. actual investment will be higher than intended investment.
    c. actual investment will be equal to intended investment.
    d. the economy is in equilibrium.
    e. to move toward equilibrium, national income must increase.

13. Changes in the equilibrium level of national income should be expected because
    a. consumption changes frequently.
    b. saving changes frequently.
    c. investment is fairly volatile.
    d. the multiplier is quite large.
    e. the rounds of spending in the multiplier keep increasing.

14. If autonomous investment decreases by $200 billion and if the marginal propensity to consume is 0.75, then national income will
    a. rise by $200 billion.
    b. fall by $200 billion.
    c. fall by $267 billion.
    d. rise by $267 billion.
    e. fall by $800 billion.

15. An increase in the marginal propensity to save from 0.20 to 0.50 means that
    a. the marginal propensity to consume falls from 0.80 to 0.50.
    b. less is saved at every level of national income.
    c. more is consumed at every level of national income.
    d. the marginal propensity to consume increases as well from 0.20 to 0.50.
    e. intended investment increases by 30 percent.

16. The paradox in the paradox of thrift is that as people try to save more
    a. aggregate expenditures increase.
    b. national income increases.
    c. investment increases.
    d. income decreases and saving doesn't change.
    e. income increases and saving doesn't change.

*17. An increase in exports causes aggregate expenditures to
    a. rise.
    b. fall.
    c. multiply.
    d. shift down.
    e. flow toward imported goods and services.

*18. When exports equals imports
    a. national income increases by a multiple of the value of exports and imports.
    b. national income decreases by a multiple of the value of exports and imports.
    c. C + I = C + I + (net exports).
    d. the marginal propensity to consume increases.
    e. the marginal propensity to consume decreases.

19. When the income multiplier works in reverse (is negative)
    a. the change in investment must have been negative.
    b. the marginal propensity to consume must have fallen.
    c. the marginal propensity to save must have fallen.
    d. the consumption curve must have risen.
    e. employment must increase.

20. When the level of consumption equals the level of national income
    a. the economy is in equilibrium.
    b. autonomous consumption must be zero.
    c. aggregate expenditures is equal to intended investment.
    d. saving is zero.
    e. saving equals consumption.

Problems

1. a. Suppose that the consumption function is $C = 80 + .8Y$ and the income level is $1,400 billion. Calculate what consumers intend to consume and save at this income level.

   b. Suppose that at an income level of $1,400 billion producers intend to produce $1,300 billion of consumption and intend to invest $100 billion. Is the economy in equilibrium? Explain, using a graph to aid discussion.

   c. If this economy is not in equilibrium, what would the equilibrium level of national income be, assuming that intended investment remains at $100 billion? How does the economy adjust to the new equilibrium?

2. Suppose an economy is described by the following equations: $C = \$100 + 0.75Y$ and $I = \$300$.

   a. Calculate the equilibrium level of income.

   b. Graph the aggregate expenditures curve and the 45° line.

c. Suppose saving increases by $50 at every level of national income. How would the aggregate expenditures curve you drew be affected? Explain. Calculate the new equilibrium level of national income.

d. Calculate the level of saving at the original equilibrium and at the new equilibrium. Does this example demonstrate the paradox of thrift? Explain.

Discussion Questions

1. What is the difference between actual and intended investment?

2. Why doesn't an increase in aggregate expenditures cause the price level to increase in the Keynesian model?

3. Explain the logic of the multiplier.

4. Why don't increases in saving automatically translate into increased investment in the Keynesian model?

Answers to Questions

True-False Questions

1. False because intended saving and investment are only equal in equilibrium.
2. True
3. True
4. False because aggregate expenditure is equal to consumption plus investment.
5. True
6. False because an increase in autonomous investment causes national income to increase by a multiple.
7. False because an increase and decrease in autonomous investment will have equal and opposite effects.
8. True
9. False because as the marginal propensity to consume increases so does the income multiplier.
10. True
11. False because inventories will be unchanged.
12. True
13. True
14. False because the income multiplier is equal to 1/1 − mpc.
15. True
16. True
*17. True
*18. False because our exports to these countries would be falling.
*19. True
*20. True

Multiple Choice Questions

1. d	6. a	11. a	16. d
2. c	7. a	12. b	*17. a
3. c	8. b	13. c	*18. c
4. b	9. b	14. e	*19. a
5. b	10. c	15. a	*20. d

Problems

1. a. Consumers intend to consume $1,200 billion and save $200 billion.

   b. This economy is not in equilibrium because $100 billion of unwanted inventories will accumulate.

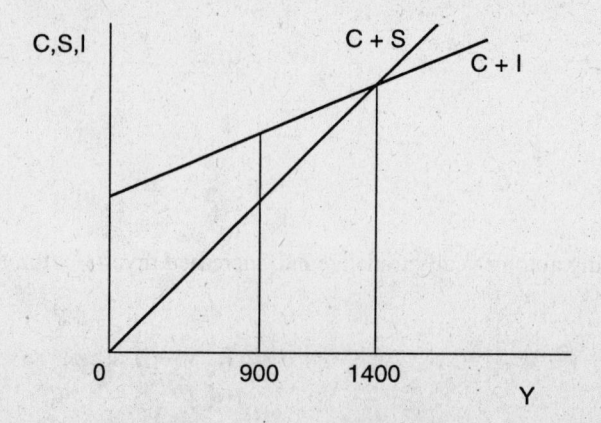

c. The equilibrium is $900 billion and the economy adjusts to this equilibrium as inventories increase and production, employment, and income decrease from the $1,400 level.

2. a. The equilibrium level of income is calculated by setting Y = $100 + 0.75Y + $300 and solving for Y which is $1,600.

b-c. An increase in saving is represented by a downward shift in the aggregate expenditures curve of $50 in this case. The equilibrium level of income decreases to $1,400. These changes are shown in the graph. Aggregate expenditures falls from C + I to C' + I and the equilibrium level of income falls from $1,600 to $1,400.

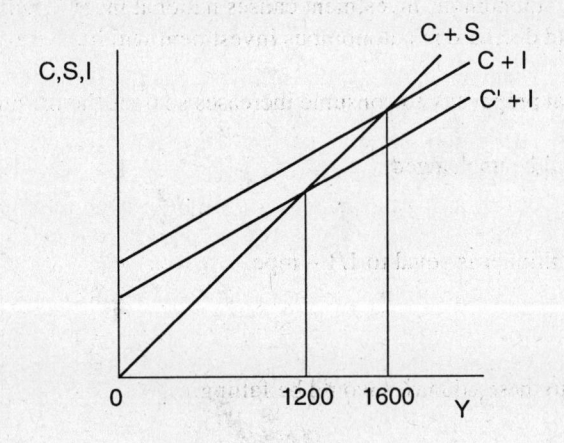

d. Saving is equal to $300 at both levels of income.

Discussion Questions

1. Actual investment includes unwanted changes in inventories.

2. The price level is assumed to be constant.

3. The logic behind the multiplier is that an increase in autonomous spending becomes someone's income and consumption, which becomes someone else's income and consumption, and so on. Each successive round of incomes is reduced by the marginal propensity to save.

4. Because the people doing the saving are not the same as the people doing the investment. There is no automatic coordination or match of saving and investment.

CHAPTER 8

FISCAL POLICY: COPING WITH INFLATION AND UNEMPLOYMENT

Chapter Summary

To say that an economy is in equilibrium tells us very little about the general state of the economy. Keynes' model allows for an economy to be in equilibrium at high levels of unemployment. Some of the unemployment is caused by an insufficiency in aggregate expenditures.

But there are other causes of unemployment. Economists identify five types: frictional unemployment, structural unemployment, cyclical unemployment, discouraged workers, and the underemployed. Frictional refers to those who voluntarily quit to seek a better job. Structural refers to those who lost a job through technological displacement. Cyclical refers to those laid off during downturn and recession phases of the business cycle. Discouraged workers refer to those who have given up trying to find a job. Underemployed refer to those who are working but at jobs well below their capabilities.

The Bureau of Labor Statistics, which sets the official unemployment count and rate of unemployment for the economy, calculates the rate of unemployment by surveying households. Those who are either working or seeking employment are counted in the labor force. That excludes discouraged workers. The unemployment rate is the number of people who are not working but seeking work, divided by the labor force.

Economists differentiate between that rate and the actual rate of unemployment. The difference is accounted for by the *natural rate of unemployment.* The natural rate of unemployment consists of workers who are frictionally and structurally unemployed. It is "natural" and the result of positive dynamic forces in the economy—people looking for better jobs and technological change occurring—so that the natural rate is not at all worrisome. What remains is cyclical unemployment, which the BLS defines as the actual rate.

Full employment exists when the unemployment rate is equal to the natural rate. In the Keynesian version of the aggregate supply and aggregate demand model, full employment occurs when the quantity of aggregate demand intersects the quantity of aggregate supply on the vertical segment of the aggregate supply curve. In the modified version, real GDP and employment are related to the price level. When the price level (and wages) increases, employment increases up to a point where the aggregate supply curve becomes vertical. In order to reach full employment, some inflation must be tolerated.

When inflation occurs, some groups of people are harmed while others benefit. Those who are hurt by inflation include people living on fixed incomes, such as landlords, and savers. Those who gain from inflation include borrowers and, to some extent, the government. The government benefits from inflation when it borrows. Unions bargain for cost of living allowances in their wage contracts to protect themselves from the erosion of real wages.

What's the relationship between the full employment level of national income and the equilibrium level? A *recessionary gap* exists when the equilibrium level of national income falls below the full employment level. The amount by which spending must increase in order to achieve full employment defines the recessionary gap. An *inflationary gap* exists when the equilibrium level of national income is above the full employment level. The inflationary gap defines the amount by which spending must decrease in order to achieve full employment without inflation.

How do you close these gaps? A recessionary gap can be closed by government spending. When the government spends, the income multiplier kicks in, and national income arises. But government spending is not without its problems. For example, government spending, once introduced, may be hard to withdraw. Also, it feeds the budget deficit. Many economists are concerned about government spending to close a recessionary gap because they believe that the economy, given sufficient time, would adjust to full employment automatically. If insufficient investment demand is the problem, then over time, depreciation and new technologies will induce firms to increase investment, which will lead to a multiple expansion in income.

Conversely, inflationary gaps can be closed by cuts in government spending. The problem here is that the needed cuts would not be easy to implement because those who would be directly hurt by the cuts would oppose them. The government, a political as well as an economic institution, is highly sensitive to voter dissatisfaction.

Fiscal policy—how government uses its budget to close recessionary and inflationary gaps—involves not only government increasing or decreasing its spending but increasing or decreasing its tax take. Just as an increase in government spending creates a multiple increase in national income, an increase in taxes creates a multiple decrease in national income. After all, more taxes mean less spending by the taxpayers. The tax multiplier is $-MPC/(1-MPC)$. When the government increases its spending and taxes by the same amount, both the income and tax multipliers are at work. The net effect is an increase in national income that equals the increase in spending and taxes. *The balanced budget multiplier* is one.

The government can create a balanced budget where $G = T$, a surplus budget where $T>G$, or a deficit budget where $G>T$. The government can exercise a variety of fiscal policy options—different combinations of G and T.

Not all economists accept the Keynesian idea that fiscal policy can be an effective tool for bringing the equilibrium level of national income to its full employment level, without inflation. Other competing theories will be examined in later chapters.

Key Terms — Test your comprehension by defining and explaining the significance of these terms.

frictional unemployment
structural unemployment
cyclical unemployment
discouraged workers
underemployed workers
labor force
natural rate of unemployment
full employment

recessionary gap
inflationary gap
fiscal policy
balanced budget
tax multiplier
balanced budget multiplier
budget deficit
budget surplus

True-False Questions — If a statement is false, explain why.

1. Keynesians believe that the economy moves toward equilibrium at full employment. (T/F)

2. The reason that the economy may be at an equilibrium below full employment is because prices are inflexible. (T/F)

3. The upward-sloping segment of the aggregate supply curve shows that increases in real GDP can only occur with increases in the price level. (T/F)

4. An inflationary gap can be closed by cutting taxes. (T/F)

5. The actual rate of unemployment is described as natural when the rate of cyclical unemployment is zero. (T/F)

6. According to Keynesians, reducing the budget's deficit closes a recessionary gap while increasing the deficit closes an inflationary gap. (T/F)

7. Structural unemployment is included in the natural rate of unemployment. (T/F)

8. Discouraged workers are not counted in the natural rate of unemployment but are included in the actual rate of unemployment. (T/F)

9. Banks that provide loans to businesses and individuals are losers during periods of high inflation. (T/F)

10. People living on fixed income, such as retirees, are harmed by inflation. (T/F)

11. According to Keynesians, an increase in government spending can close or eliminate a recessionary gap, depending on the size of the gap and the size of the government spending. (T/F)

12. According to Keynesians, an increase in government spending generates an increase in national income just as an increase in private investment spending would. (T/F)

13. Closing a recessionary gap using deficit financing requires less government spending than financing the closing with a balanced budget. (T/F)

14. A deficit budget results when tax revenues are greater than the government's spending. (T/F)

15. The tax multiplier is always larger than the income multiplier. (T/F)

16. National income will increase by exactly the amount that government spending increases if there are tax increases to match the government spending increases. (T/F)

17. Critics of the Keynesian view argue that even if government did nothing to counteract a recessionary gap, the gap would still close because investment spending would eventually increase in response to falling wage rates, capital depreciation, and technological change. (T/F)

18. Balancing the budget, even at increased levels, reduces the government's role in the economy. (T/F)

19. It's a package deal: If you adopt a tax-free policy to close a recessionary gap, you end up with a deficit budget. (T/F)

20. Picture the aggregate demand and aggregate supply model: The closer the economy comes to full employment by way of deficit financing, the more it must accept higher levels in the price level. (T/F)

Multiple Choice Questions

1. The economy is considered to be at full employment when the rate of _____ is zero.
   a. cyclical unemployment
   b. seasonal unemployment
   c. frictional unemployment
   d. structural unemployment
   e. discouraged workers

2. When a balanced budget increases by $120 billion, national income increases by
   a. $60 billion.
   b. $120 billion.
   c. $240 billion.
   d. $600 billion.
   e. national income does not increase.

3. An inflationary gap closes with
   a. increasing investments by producers.
   b. increases in government spending.
   c. tax cuts.
   d. increases in consumption spending.
   e. cuts in government spending.

4. Of the different types of unemployment, the one associated with technological displacement of labor is
   a. cyclical.
   b. structural.
   c. frictional.
   d. discouraged workers.
   e. underemployed workers.

5. The economy is at full employment when
   a. there are no discouraged workers.
   b. the actual rate of unemployment equals the natural rate.
   c. there is no frictional unemployment.
   d. the economy is in equilibrium.
   e. everyone over the age of 21 is employed.

6. All of the following groups are harmed by inflation except
   a. retirees.
   b. minimum wage workers.
   c. landlords.
   d. lenders.
   e. renters.

7. The type of unemployment which government policy is best suited to control is
   a. natural.
   b. structural.
   c. discouraged.
   d. cyclical.
   e. frictional.

8. According to the Bureau of Labor Statistics (BLS), all of the following make up the labor force except
   a. discouraged workers.
   b. underemployed workers.
   c. frictionally unemployed workers.
   d. cyclically unemployed workers.
   e. structurally unemployed workers.

9. People who are on fixed incomes are adversely affected by inflation because
   a. their incomes buy fewer goods and services.
   b. while their income may increase with inflation, it increases at a lower rate than the rate of inflation.
   c. they typically have large outstanding debts like a mortgage.
   d. the minimum wage which they receive does not increase.
   e. they are unable to pick the cheaper goods and services to buy like they did before the inflation.

10. A $100 billion deficit results from a(n)
    a. increase in G by $140 billion and an increase in T by $40 billion.
    b. increase in G by $140 billion and an increase in T by $140 billion.
    c. decrease in G by $140 billion and an increase in T by $40 billion.
    d. decrease in G by $140 billion and a decrease in T by $140 billion.
    e. decrease in G by $40 billion and an increase in T by $100 billion.

11. Suppose national income is $2,000 billion and the full employment level is $2,400 billion. Given a marginal propensity to consume equal to 0.80, the amount by which taxes must change in order to reach full employment is
    a. $80 billion.
    b. –$80 billion.
    c. –$400 billion.
    d. $100 billion.
    e. –$100 billion.

12. Given the same information as in question 11, the amount by which government spending and taxes must change to reach full employment is
    a. increase G by $240 billion and decrease T by $200 billion.
    b. decrease G by $240 billion and increase T by $200 billion.
    c. decrease G by $240 billion and decrease T by $200 billion.
    d. increase G by $240 billion and increase T by $200 billion.
    e. increase G by $200 billion and increase T by $160 billion.

13. If the government policy creates a deficit budget while the economy is already at full employment, then
    a. national income is falling.
    b. fiscal policy is inflationary.
    c. fiscal policy is recessionary.
    d. the balanced budget multiplier must be less than one.
    e. the balanced budget multiplier must be greater than one.

14. The tax multiplier is
    a. 1/MPS.
    b. −MPC/(1−MPC).
    c. −1/(1−MPC).
    d. MPS/(1−MPS).
    e. T−G/(1+T).

15. The balanced budget multiplier is
    a. greater than one when national income is increasing.
    b. less than one when national income is increasing.
    c. less than one when national income is decreasing.
    d. equal to one whether national income increases or decreases.
    e. equal to one only when G=T=1.

16. If the income multiplier is 4, government spending must increase by _____ and taxes by _____ to generate a $300 increase in national income.
    a. $250; $200
    b. $150; $100
    c. $200; $200
    d. $200; $250
    e. $300; $250

17. A frictionally unemployed person is one who
    a. quit a job in order to find a better one.
    b. has retired from a job.
    c. lost a job due to a technological change in the production process.
    d. lost a job due to a downturn or recession phase in the economy.
    e. takes a job which requires considerably less talent than that person has to offer.

18. A surplus budget arises when
    a. the balanced budget multiplier generates a level of national income greater than the full employment level.
    b. tax revenues exceed government spending.
    c. the tax multiplier is greater than the income multiplier.
    d. the income multiplier is greater than the tax multiplier.
    e. the tax increase necessary to balance the budget is more than the increase in government spending.

19. Fiscal policy refers to
    a. the practice of balancing the budget.
    b. creating budgets—surplus, deficit or balanced—to achieve desired results.
    c. recessionary and inflationary gaps.
    d. income and tax multipliers.
    e. achieving an equilibrium level of national income.

20. Given a $10 billion recessionary gap and MPC = 0.75, we know that the equilibrium level of national income is
    a. $40 billion below the full employment level of national income.
    b. $30 billion below the full employment level of national income.
    c. $50 billion above the full employment level of national income.
    d. $30 billion above the full employment level of national income.
    e. at full employment.

Problems

1. Graph a recessionary gap and an inflationary gap.

2. Suppose that the full employment level of national income is $2,000 billion, the equilibrium level of national income is $1,600 billion, and the marginal propensity to consume is 0.75. By how much will spending have to increase in order to reach full employment?

3. Suppose that the full employment level of national income is $2,000 billion and the equilibrium level of national income is $2,500 billion. By how much will taxes have to change given a marginal propensity to consume equal to 0.80 in order to reach full employment?

4. Create a $20 billion surplus budget to close the inflationary gap you calculated in question 3. What changes in government spending and taxes will accomplish this goal?

Discussion Questions

1. Suppose that the economy is below full employment. Is it necessary to introduce an expansionary fiscal policy in order to eliminate the recessionary gap? Explain.

2. Define the unemployment rate. Does the definition include all the people of working age who don't have jobs? Explain.

3. Why do bankers lose in inflation?

4. Which is the most difficult type of unemployment to eliminate and why?

5. Why is the balanced budget multiplier equal to one?

Answers to Questions

True-False Questions

1. False because the economy does not necessarily move to a full employment equilibrium.
2. True
3. True
4. False because a recessionary gap could be cured by cutting taxes.
5. True
6. False because closing a recessionary gap requires an increase in the deficit while closing an inflationary gap requires a surplus budget.
7. True
8. False because discouraged workers are not counted in the unemployed or labor force.
9. True
10. True
11. True
12. True
13. True
14. False because a deficit budget means greater spending than taxes.
15. False because the income multiplier is bigger.
16. True
17. True
18. False because government's role would expand.
19. True
20. True

Multiple Choice Questions

1. a
2. b
3. e
4. b
5. b
6. e
7. d
8. a
9. a
10. a
11. e
12. d
13. b
14. b
15. d
16. b
17. a
18. b
19. b
20. a

Problems

1. These sketches are shown here. The first one shows the recessionary gap as the vertical distance between the AE and AE'. The second drawing shows the inflationary gap as the vertical distance between AE and AE".

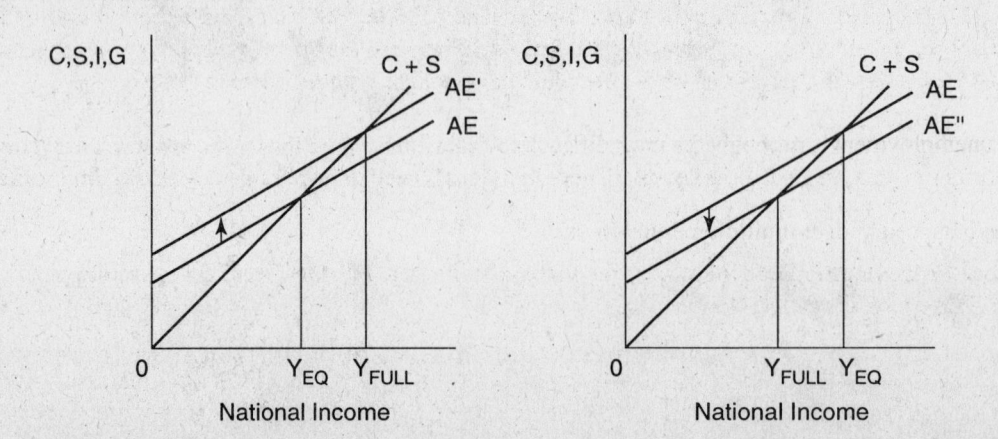

2. The change in national income required in this case is $400 billion. The multiplier is 4. Therefore, the change in spending required is $100 billion.

3. The change in national income required is -$500 billion. The tax multiplier is –4. Therefore, taxes must increase by $125 billion in order to reach full employment.

4. The difference between changes in government spending and taxes is –$20 billion. That is, the change in government spending minus the change in taxes is equal to –$20 billion. We can write this as an equation

$$-20 = \Delta G - \Delta T$$

The income multiplier is 5 and the tax multiplier is –4. Therefore, the change in national income is the difference between five times the change in government spending and four times the change in taxes. We can write this as an equation

$$\Delta Y = 5\Delta G - 4\Delta T$$

Rearranging the first equation, we have the following expression—

$$\Delta T = \Delta G + 20$$

Substituting in the second equation for T,

$$\Delta Y = 5\Delta G - 4(\Delta G - 20).$$

Solving for ΔG, we get $\Delta G = -420$ so that ΔT must be -400.

Discussion Questions

1. According to Keynesians, it would. Other economists believe it may not be necessary because eventually the economy will adjust on its own back to full employment. For example, there may be a change in technology that prompts many entrepreneurs to invest in new capital equipment that prompts an increase in aggregate expenditures. Or, it may be that old capital simply wears out, causing an increase in investment. The drawback to such automatic adjustment is that it may take a very long time.

2. The unemployment rate is the percentage of the labor force that is looking for work. This definition does not include all people of working age who don't have jobs. Some people of working age are not in the labor force so they can't be unemployed. Discouraged workers are not included in this group.

3. Bankers lend money and are repaid in the future. If they lend $100 in 1990 and receive the full loan of $100 back in 1995 but, in the five intervening years, inflation totaled 50 percent, the quantity of goods and services that $100 buys the bankers is only 50 percent of what they could have bought with the $100 in 1990.

4. Structural unemployment is probably the most difficult to deal with because those who are structurally unemployed don't possess skills that are easily marketable. These individuals need to be retrained, which is time consuming and costly.

5. The balanced budget multiplier is the sum of the income multiplier, 1/1–MPC, and the tax multiplier, –MPC/1–MPC, which is equal to 1.

CHAPTER 9

ECONOMIC GROWTH, BUSINESS CYCLES, AND COUNTERCYCLICAL FISCAL POLICY

Chapter Summary

Up to this point in our analysis of macroeconomics, our focus has been on understanding why the economy is either in or moving toward equilibrium. We looked at the relationship between the economy's equilibrium level of national income and its full employment level. We studied how government, through its fiscal policy, can achieve an equilibrium level at full employment, without causing much, if any, inflation. We also considered the criticisms of this Keynesian approach.

This chapter presents a very different approach to macroeconomic analysis. It drops the idea that the economy moves incessantly toward equilibrium. Instead, it describes an economy always in motion, moving from one level of activity to another, never heading toward a particular position, yet not altogether wandering. The point of reference in this somewhat different approach to macroeconomics—although we use pretty much the same concepts we used in macroequilibrium analysis—is the business cycle. The economy is always somewhere on the business cycle, moving from one phase to another. The phases, which we discussed in earlier chapters, are recession (bottom of the cycle), recovery, prosperity (peak of the cycle), and downturn.

But let's not get ahead of ourselves. The chapter opens with a discussion of economic growth. Being on a business cycle is not inconsistent with economic growth if, cycle after cycle, the economy's level of activity—its real GDP—increases. And that, indeed, has been our experience. What causes growth? Increases in the size of the labor force, with its specialization and division of labor, increases in the stock of capital, and improvements in technology explain the approximate 3.5 percent annual rate of growth in the U.S. economy over the years 1900 to 1990. Table 1 in the text shows the importance of each to the growth process. A simple model of growth, dependent on changes in capital stock, shows how changes in capital translate into changes in real output.

Figure 1 in the text shows that although the U.S. economy grew by approximately 3.5 percent per year during the 20th century, the ride up the real GDP scale was by no means smooth. Its twists and turns were, at times, traumatic, as in the case of the Great Depression of the 1930s. Economists have tried to figure out why the economy is subject to these twists and turns. That is to say: Why the business cycle? Business cycle theorists offer a number of explanations, each of which can be viewed as belonging to either of two classes: externally-induced cycles or internally-induced cycles.

Externally-induced cycles refer to those triggered by causes that are external to the economy, such as wars, changes in climate, population booms, clustering of innovations, changes in consumer confidence, changes in government spending, or changes in the international scene. The chapter describes Jevons' sunspot theory, which ascribes changes in economic activity to changes in the number of sunspots in our solar system. War-induced cycles link prosperity to war preparedness and the downturn to the consequences of peace. Population-induced cycles link prosperity to the heightened demands for goods and services caused by a baby boom. The housing cycle ties prosperity to housing starts, and the innovation cycle traces the connection between prosperity and extraordinary investments caused by a clustering of interrelating new technologies.

The internally-induced cycle supposes that the economy is inherently cyclical. One theory that explains such an internally-induced cycle shows how the multiplier and accelerator interact to create the cycle. Remember: The multiplier relates changes in investment to changes in income. The accelerator relates the level of investment to changes in income. A cycle can be triggered by a change in investment that changes income (the multiplier at work). That change in income changes the level of investment (the accelerator at work). That second round change in investment changes income (second round multiplier at work), and so on.

Not all economists accept the idea of the business cycle. Real business cycle theorists believe that there is no such thing as a business cycle marked by regular and distinct phases. Rather, the economy is highly dynamic operating at full employment. What others diagnose as business cycles are, to them, really just sharp changes in the rate of economic growth. Economic growth rates are highly random because technological changes are random.

Countercyclical fiscal policy can be used to moderate both the downturns and prosperity phases of the cycle. The appropriate fiscal policy response to a downturn is to create a budget deficit by either raising government spending or lowering taxes, or both. To counteract inflationary pressures in the prosperity phase, the government should cut its spending, raise taxes, or both. While it may appear to be appropriate policy, it is not always effective. This is because it is not always clear where in the cycle the economy is positioned, or where it is heading. Anticipating the cycle's turning points is, at best, guesswork. Moreover, even if it was clear what policy measure to use, there is still an administrative lag to overcome. The lag is the time interval between deciding on a policy and the execution of that policy. By the time it clears through the lag, it may no longer be appropriate.

Key Terms — Test your comprehension by defining and explaining the significance of these terms.

economic growth   accelerator
labor productivity   countercyclical fiscal policy
capital/output ratio   administrative lag

True-False Questions — If a statement is false, explain why.

1. National income equilibrium is more a theoretical construct than an observable reality. (T/F)

2. From 1900 to 1990, average annual real GDP growth in the U.S. was about 3.5 percent. (T/F)

3. Our ideas about the causes of economic growth are much different today from those that were advanced by Adam Smith in 1776. (T/F)

4. The capital-output ratio tells us how many dollars' worth of capital are required to generate a dollar's worth of output. (T/F)

5. The model of economic growth based on the linkage between capital stock and GDP incorporates all the key factors associated with the growth process. (T/F)

6. Technological change contributed relatively less to economic growth in the period 1947–1973 than it did in the period 1973–1992. (T/F)

7. During the 20th century, the U.S. economic growth path traces out a steady, upward thrust in real GDP. (T/F)

8. There is a universal consensus among economists that business cycles exist. (T/F)

9. The sunspot theory associated movements through a business cycle with changes in solar activity. (T/F)

10. Marxists argue that wars are used by governments as a means to overcome economic recessions or depressions. (T/F)

11. The baby boom of the 1960s was the mainspring of investments that triggered a population-driven business cycle. (T/F)

12. Creative destruction refers to the real business cycle, which its proponents argue results from new technologies that cause some industries to flourish and others to decay. (T/F)

13. The multiplier-accelerator cycle is based on the premise that the economy is inherently cyclical. (T/F)

14. The accelerator principle suggests that an increase in national income will induce a higher level of investment. (T/F)

15. Real business cycle theorists argue that what other economists believe to be the business cycle is really just variations in the rate of economic growth attributable to uneven changes in the rate of technological change. (T/F)

16. An administrative lag refers to the time interval between deciding on appropriate policy and the execution of that policy. (T/F)

17. Countercyclical fiscal policy becomes a more effective tool as the administrative lag increases. (T/F)

Multiple Choice Questions

1. The Keynesian model focuses on _____ as the principle explanatory variable determining macroeconomic equilibrium.
   a. government spending
   b. the price level
   c. employment
   d. foreign exchange
   e. aggregate demand

2. Determinants of economic growth, according to Adam Smith, include the following, except the
   a. size of labor force.
   b. size of capital stock.
   c. rate of inflation.
   d. degree of labor specialization.
   e. level of technology.

3. The accelerator is
   a. the relationship between the level of investment and changes in the level of national income.
   b. the reciprocal of the multiplier.
   c. the rate of economic growth in the recovery phase of a business cycle.
   d. the relationship between changes in investment that cause changes in national income.
   e. the quickness in which policy decisions respond to changes in the economy.

4. The capital-output ratio
   a. describes how changes in investment affect the level of output in an economy.
   b. describes how the level of investment affects changes in the economy's output.
   c. describes the relationship between the economy's capital stock and its output.
   d. is the key factor explaining why business cycles develop in a capitalized economy.
   e. measures changes in output during one cycle, from peak to recession.

5. William Stanley Jevons' sunspot theory relates
   a. economic performance to nuclear storms on the sun.
   b. investment behavior of firms to seasons of the year.
   c. changes in consumers' propensities to consume to seasons of the year.
   d. change in economic performance to government's fiscal policy.
   e. changes in economic performance to changes in the interest rate.

6. The real business cycle theory claims that
   a. business cycles occur because the economy is not competitive.
   b. economic performance is linked to technological change which is totally random.
   c. competition causes business cycles.
   d. there are no adequate theories explaining why the economy experiences business cycles.
   e. downturn phases of the cycle dominate the recovery phases.

7. All of the following applies to the multiplier-accelerator model of the business cycle except
   a. the level of investment depends upon changes in national income which depend upon changes in investment.
   b. the cycle is internally fueled, that is, it is inherent to the economic system.
   c. the cycle dampens to a steady-state equilibrium in the long run.
   d. the cycle, once triggered, will repeat.
   e. it is not dependent on some external shock to the economic system, such as a war or population boom.

8. In Schumpeter's innovation cycle
   a. technological change dampens the cycle, forcing the economy to equilibrium.
   b. government's randomly distributed investments in research and development trigger the cycle.
   c. innovations cause uneven changes in labor productivity which trigger the cycle.
   d. clusters of innovations propel an economy into prosperity then, once exhausted, create the downturn.
   e. innovations cause nominal GDP to depart from real GDP which triggers the cycle.

9. Most of the increase in GDP from 1947 to 1973 is explained by _____ while _____ explains most of the growth from 1973 to 1992.
   a. technological change; capital accumulation
   b. capital accumulation; increases in the labor force
   c. increases in the labor force; capital accumulation
   d. increases in the labor force; technological change
   e. technological change; increases in the labor force

10. War-induced cycles, sunspot induced cycles, the housing cycle, and population-based cycles have this in common:
    a. they are triggered by misguided government policy.
    b. they all occur during the prosperity phase of the cycle.
    c. they are internally-induced; that is, each occurs because they are an integral part of the economic system.
    d. their causes are external to the economic system.
    e. they are all by-products of the multiplier-accelerator cycle.

11. The textbook argues that the Great Depression may reflect
    a. a one-time severe downturn in a typical business cycle caused by an unusually large disinvestment in the economy.
    b. the compounding of failed government policies to correct a minor downturn in the economy.
    c. an extended administrative lag that triggered its own demise.
    d. the result of several moderate cycles whose phases, by chance, were synchronized.
    e. what real business cycle theorists describe as a multiplier-accelerator cycle "gone wild."

12. The Kuznets cycle describes
    a. the relationship between cycles and housing construction.
    b. volatile changes in the production of Kuznets, a variant of crude steel used in 19th century Russia.
    c. the relationship between changes in the real interest rate and changes in output.
    d. how the economy's marginal propensity to consume can, by itself, generate cycles.
    e. how immigration can trigger production booms in the economy that are soon followed by recession.

13. Countercyclical fiscal policy is designed to
    a. moderate the severity of the business cycle.
    b. create a balanced budget in each of the years of a cycle.
    c. counter fiscal policies that create deficits which trigger cycles.
    d. curb the excessive powers of government's fiscal policy on cycles.
    e. create a cycle whose phases are of equal length.

14. An administrative lag
    a. reflects differences in the government's willingness to cope with inflation and unemployment.
    b. is the time it takes fiscal policy to clear the bureaucratic channels of government.
    c. is the time interval between making a fiscal policy decision and the actual execution of that policy.
    d. the time interval between executing and later correcting inappropriate fiscal policy.
    e. measures the number of government agencies required to approve any policy.

15. A problem inherent in creating countercyclical fiscal policy when the economy is in a downturn is
    a. the private sector may not go along with that policy, thus undermining the effort.
    b. competition among firms in the economy creates a less-than-uniform response to any government policy.
    c. government agencies fight among themselves—some want to curb unemployment, others inflation.
    d. it is impossible to know where the economy is heading, on to recession or towards its recovery phase.
    e. lack of consumer confidence undermines any government effort to initiate the recovery phase.

Problems

1. Suppose the capital-output ratio is 4 and the initial level of income is $1,000. Suppose the marginal propensity to consume is 0.80. Construct a table to show the level of income, the size of the capital stock, consumption, saving and investment for a four-year period. What is the rate of growth for this economy? What allows this economy to grow?

Discussion Questions

1. Clearly, technological change is an important contributor to economic growth. However, technological change is sometimes hard to observe and nearly always hard to quantify. How then can economists go about measuring the contribution of technological change to economic growth?

2. If you were to compare the economic cycles experienced by the United States and the other industrialized economies, you would find that these cycles are closely linked to each other. Why do you suppose this is the case? That is, why would the United States and the other industrialized countries simultaneously tend to be in recession and boom?

3. How is it that economic cycles are related to the level of sunspot activity? Would you be comfortable predicting economic performance in the United States over the next five years based on sunspot activity? Why or why not?

4. Explain the innovation cycle.

5. What is the difference between autonomous and induced investment?

6. How does real business cycle theory compare to the theory of the long-wave innovation cycle?

7. Describe circumstances under which a countercyclical fiscal policy could be destabilizing even though it was the right thing to do when the policy was introduced.

Answers to Questions

True-False Questions

1. True
2. True
3. False because Smith identified the same principal factors that we study today as the sources of economic growth.
4. True
5. False because economic growth is a function of many other factors, such as labor input and technological change.
6. False because technological change was relatively more important in the early period.
7. False because this period is marked by major fluctuations in real GDP.
8. False because some economists completely reject the idea of a business cycle.
9. True
10. True
11. True
12. False because creative destruction is associated with the long-wave innovation cycle.
13. True
14. True
15. True
16. True
17. False because increases in the lag make the policy less effective.

Multiple Choice Questions

1. e
2. c
3. a
4. c
5. a
6. b
7. c
8. d
9. a
10. d
11. d
12. a
13. a
14. c
15. d

Problem

1. The table with the computations is shown here. This economy is growing at a five percent per year rate. Ultimately, it is saving that leads to investment and capital accumulation that allows this economy to grow.

	Y	K	C	S	I
Yr. 1	1000	4000	800	200	200
Yr. 2	1050	4200	840	210	210
Yr. 3	1102.5	4410	881.6	220.9	220.9
Yr. 4	1157.725	4630.9	926.18	231.545	231.545

Discussion Questions

1. This is a difficult question. Economists calculate the percent of the economy's rate of growth that can be attributed to increases in the labor force and increases in the capital stock. The residual, unexplained percent is attributed, at least in part, to technological change.

2. The industrialized countries trade extensively with each other. When one of the economies is in recession—aggregate expenditures, incomes and employment falling—it buys less from the others, which lowers their aggregate expenditures, incomes and employment. It is no surprise than that their economic performances are linked.

3. High levels of sunspot activity seem to be related to poor crop performance. This theory of the business cycle wouldn't be good for predicting cycles in the United States because such a small portion of our GDP is accounted for by agriculture. However, in the 19th century, when a larger percentage of the population farmed for a living, this theory made some sense and perhaps had some explanatory power.

4. The innovation cycle refers to technological changes that are clustered in particular industries which lead to high rates of investment in these industries. These innovations spurt the economy into prosperity. When the innovations run their course, and the level of innovative activity falls, the economy slips into its downturn phase. A good example is the progress of transportation technology during the 19th century and into the 20th. New technologies and new industries replaced old ones as the automobile replaced the train and so on. These waves of investment can cause an economic cycle.

5. Changes in autonomous investment are unrelated to levels of income or changes in the levels of national income. Induced investment, on the other hand, occurs in response to changes in the level of national income.

6. Real business cycle theorists don't believe in a business cycle. Rather, they argue that the economy experiences periodic bursts of rapid growth associated with rapid technological changes that are randomly occurring in the economy. On the other hand, the innovation cycle focuses on technological changes that are significant enough to lead to major changes in investment, which starts the cycle process.

7. Suppose the economy was in recession and the President, hoping to moderate the economy's decline, decides on a massive spending program. By the time the program is approved by Congress, the economy has begun its recovery. But the program now takes affect and instead of moderating the economy's fall, contributes to the growing inflationary pressures.

CHAPTER 10

MONEY

Chapter Summary

Although we know from experience that, under certain circumstances, barter exchange works—goods for goods—the complications associated with the requirements of a double coincidence of wants makes barter exchange inappropriate in the modern world. Money was invented to facilitate exchange. Money serves three functions. It is a medium of exchange, a measure of value, and a store of value. What properties must money have? It must be durable, portable, divisible, homogenous, and be relatively scarce. Gold has these characteristics and has been used as money from time immemorial. Paper money—called fiat money—works as well, as long as it is universally accepted as the medium of exchange.

Let's look at our modern world of money. Money is described as a liquid asset because it exchanges easily for other assets. Our money supply is categorized according to its liquidity. M1 is the most liquid. It includes currency and demand deposits (our checking accounts) and traveler's checks. M2 is M1 money plus savings accounts, certificates of deposit, money market mutual funds, money market deposit accounts, NOW accounts, share-draft accounts, and ATS accounts. M3 is M2 money plus other less liquid forms of money such as large denomination time deposits and overnight repurchase agreements.

Consider the most inclusive form of money: M3. In 1993, M3 money supply was $4,172 billion. Our currency amounts to less than 10 percent of M3 money. Almost 50 percent of our money is in savings and small time accounts. The money supply grew rapidly in the 1970s when people left the stock market to invest in money market mutual funds and money market deposit accounts, part of M2 money. When economists refer to the money supply, they are usually referring to M1.

The relationship between an economy's prices and its money supply is expressed in the quantity theory of money which derives from the equation of exchange: $MV = PQ$, where M is the money supply, V is the velocity of money, P is the price level, and Q the quantity of goods. The quantity theory of money restates the equation to read: $P = MV/Q$. We now see the direct relationship between money and prices (increase money, the price level increases) and the inverse relationship between goods (or real GDP) and prices (increase goods, the price level falls). What about the velocity of money?

Economists hold different views concerning the velocity of money. Classical economists believe velocity is constant; monetarists believe it is not constant but stable and predictable; and Keynesians believe it is not only not constant but neither stable nor predictable. Economists' views on velocity affect their policy prescriptions. These show up in their theories of demand for money.

Classical economists believed that the demand for money is strictly a transactions demand, that is, a demand arising from the need to carry out transactions. They assume that since output is constant at full employment and velocity is constant, then the transactions demand for money depends on the price level. Monetarists accept variability of velocity but believe that $MV = PQ$ can still be a good tool for analysis because, even though velocity is variable, it is predictable.

Keynesians have a more complex view of money demand. They believe that there are three motives for demanding (holding) money: the transactions motive, the precautionary motive, and the speculative motive. The speculative demand for money is inversely related to the interest rate. A fall in the rate increases the quantity demanded of money. Picture the money market with a downward-sloping demand curve for money and a fixed money supply. If the money supply curve shifts to the right, interest rates will fall, setting off a domino-style reaction: Lower interest rates mean higher levels of investment, which raises aggregate demand which raises real GDP. To Keynesians, money matters. Classical economists and monetarists, on the other hand, believe that increases in the money supply cause prices to increase because the economy is continuously at full employment.

Key Terms — Test your comprehension by defining and explaining the significance of these terms.

barter	M2 money supply
money	M3 money supply
fiat money	velocity of money
currency	equation of exchange
liquidity	quantity theory of money
money	transactions demand for money
M1 money supply	

True-False Questions — If a statement is false, explain why.

1. Barter only works effectively when there is a double coincidence of wants. (T/F)

2. Gold has properties that make it a relatively good form of money. (T/F)

3. Paper money that is backed by gold is called fiat money. (T/F)

4. Our dollar bills are issued by the federal government. (T/F)

5. An asset is considered to be liquid if it can easily be exchanged for money. (T/F)

6. As one moves through the various forms of money supply—from M1, through M2, to M3—liquidity increases. (T/F)

7. Time deposits, such as people's savings accounts, are considered to be part of M1. (T/F)

8. The largest portion of our money supply is in the form of currency. (T/F)

9. The transactions demand for money refers to the amount of money necessary for people to transact the aggregate supply of goods and services. (T/F)

10. If the velocity of money is equal to one, then the transactions demand for money is equal to nominal GDP. (T/F)

11. Coins and dollar bills make up our currency. (T/F)

12. Assuming full employment and a constant velocity of money, an increase in the money supply will lead to a proportionate increase in the price level. (T/F)

13. Monetarists believe that velocity of money is highly variable and impossible to predict. (T/F)

14. The three motives that Keynesians believe influence people's demand for money are transactions, precautionary, and speculative. (T/F)

15. Keynesians argue that money velocity is neither constant nor predictable, affected, in large measure, by changes in people's expectations of future prices. (T/F)

16. The precautionary motive for holding money reflects the inability of low-income people to make rational choices between consumption and saving. (T/F)

17. As the interest rate falls, the quantity demanded of money decreases because earnings on savings accounts fall. (T/F)

18. According to Keynesians, when the economy is in recession, an increase in the money supply could decrease the interest rate and, consequently, increase the level of investment and real GDP. (T/F)

19. The quantity of money demanded to satisfy people's speculative motive decreases as the interest rate decreases. (T/F)

20. The equation of exchange is money times prices equals velocity of money times real GDP (or MP = VQ). (T/F)

Multiple Choice Questions

1. The most liquid form of money is
   a. M1.
   b. M2.
   c. M3.
   d. gold
   e. barter.

2. The creation of new financial innovations, such as NOW accounts and ATS accounts, has
   a. created distinct differentiations between M1 and M2 money.
   b. created distinct differentiations between M2 and M3 money.
   c. blurred the distinctions between M1 and M2 money.
   d. blurred the distinctions between M2 and M3 money forms.
   e. made credit cards, such as Visa and MasterCard, a new form of money.

3. In 1993, M3 was approximately _____ the value of M1.
   a. ½
   b. equal to
   c. 50 times
   d. twice
   e. 4 times

4. In order to serve as a medium of exchange, money must fulfill all of the following requirements except
   a. divisibility.
   b. homogeneity.
   c. scarcity.
   d. attractability.
   e. durability.

5. According to Keynes, the demand for money
   a. is an increasing function of the interest rate, that is, as the interest rate rises, the demand for money rises.
   b. depends on the supply of money, which is determined by the government.
   c. is based solely on the amount of money needed to transact aggregate supply.
   d. is based on people's transactions, speculative and precautionary motives for holding money.
   e. exceeds the money supply when real GDP is greater than nominal GDP.

6. All of the following statements about M1 are correct except
   a. M1, compared to M2 and M3, is the most readily available money form.
   b. M1 includes checking accounts, which are generally more liquid than savings accounts.
   c. M1 excludes currency, which is the least liquid form of money.
   d. Travelers' checks are a form of M1 money.
   e. the quantity of money ($ billions) that makes up M1 is less than the quantities that make up M2 and M3.

7. The classical model of money demand holds that the demand for money is dependent on
   a. money supply.
   b. interest rate.
   c. nominal GDP and the velocity of money.
   d. precautionary and speculative motives for holding money.
   e. changes in the velocity of money.

8. All of the following are functions of money except
   a. a medium of exchange.
   b. a measure of value.
   c. a store of value.
   d. a source of wealth.

9. The main difference between the classical school conception of money's role in the economy and the monetarist view of money is that
   a. the classical school held that the economy was very competitive while the monetarists saw the economy as dominated by monopoly power.
   b. the classical school held that velocity was variable but predictable while the monetarists argued that velocity was constant.
   c. the classical school thought that the economy was always at full employment while the monetarists argued that persistent unemployment could arise.
   d. the classical school saw money demand as solely a transactions demand while the monetarists viewed money demand as stemming from precautionary and speculative motives.
   e. the classical school held that the velocity was constant while the monetarists argued that velocity could vary over time in ways that are predictable.

10. The value of money diminishes as
    a. it becomes more divisible.
    b. society abandons gold and silver for paper currency.
    c. it becomes more plentiful relative to other goods.
    d. an economy becomes more advanced.
    e. credit cards come into widespread use.

11. If an asset is quite liquid, then it is fair to say that
    a. problems with freezing are likely in cold northern climates.
    b. its value is fluid.
    c. the rate of return on the asset is likely to be higher than if the asset were less liquid.
    d. the asset can be easily converted to, or used as, a medium of exchange.
    e. the demand for the asset will be very stable.

12. According to the classical view of the quantity theory of money
    a. an increase in the money supply causes real output to increase.
    b. velocity is highly variable in the short run.
    c. an increase in the money supply causes nominal GDP to fall.
    d. an increase in the money supply causes the price level to increase proportionately.
    e. the impact of an increase in the money supply is impossible to predict.

13. If nominal GDP is $5 trillion, and the money supply is $500 billion, then, according to the equation of exchange, the velocity of money is
    a. 5.
    b. 0.5.
    c. 10.
    d. 100.
    e. 2.5.

14. The speculative motive for holding money is shown by
    a. John holding money, waiting for stock prices to rise.
    b. John holding money, "for a rainy day."
    c. John not spending money in May because he plans to get married and honeymoon in June.
    d. John borrowing money from the local bank to finance his college education.
    e. John buying a large quantity of lottery tickets because he speculates "today's the day."

15. The precautionary motive for holding money is shown by
    a. John holding money "for a rainy day."
    b. John borrowing money from the local bank to finance his college education.
    c. John sleeping with his cash under the mattress.
    d. John not spending money in May because he plans to get married and honeymoon in June.
    e. John holding money, waiting for stock prices to rise.

16. According to Keynesians, changes in the money supply can effect real GDP in the following way:
    a. a money supply increase when the economy is at full employment.
    b. a money supply decrease when the price level increases.
    c. a money supply increase when the economy is below full employment.
    d. a money supply decrease shifts the investment curve to the left which increases real GDP.
    e. a money supply decrease creates an excess demand for holding money which raises real GDP.

17. The Keynesian view of the quantity theory of money differs from the monetarist's in this respect:
    a. monetarists do not accept the idea of a transactions demand for money.
    b. monetarists emphasize the speculative and precautionary motives for holding money.
    c. Keynesians assume a constant velocity of money.
    d. monetarists assume the velocity of money is not unstable, but highly predictable.
    e. monetarists refer to M1 rather than M2 as the quantity of money.

18. Barter exchange refers to
    a. exchange of one good for another.
    b. the equilibrium price that arises after much bargaining and bartering occur in the market.
    c. exchange of a good for a unit of currency, other than gold.
    d. exchange of a good for a unit of gold.
    e. the sum of all values buyers and sellers place on the goods exchanged in an economy during a calendar year.

19. According to Keynesians, as the interest rate decreases the quantity of money demanded increases because
    a. the opportunity cost of holding money decreases.
    b. bonds look more attractive.
    c. people are unsure of their economic futures.
    d. more people are offering money in the form of loans.
    e. real GDP falls.

20. According to classical economists, a five percent increase in the money supply coupled with a five percent increase in real GDP will create
    a. a five percent increase in the velocity of money.
    b. a five percent increase in the price level.
    c. no changes in the price level.
    d. a 25 percent increase in the price level.
    e. a 10 percent increase in the velocity of money.

Problems

1. Suppose the economy is at full employment and that consumers increase their savings causing aggregate expenditures to decrease. Explain what happens to real GDP, to the transactions demand for money and to the interest rate.

2. Using graphs, show how a decrease in the money supply could eliminate an inflationary gap.

CHAPTER 10 MONEY

Discussion Questions

1. Discuss the advantages of money over barter.

2. Does a $100 nominal GDP imply a $100 money supply? Explain.

3. What's the difference between the equation of exchange and the quantity theory of money?

4. How would the expectation of a rise in the price level affect the demand for money in the Keynesian model? What would happen to velocity if people expected a rise in the price level?

Answers to Questions

True-False Questions

1. True
2. True
3. False because fiat money is not backed by gold.
4. False because they are issued by the Federal Reserve.
5. True
6. False because M2 and M3 are less liquid than M1.
7. False because they are part of M2.
8. False because the largest part of the money supply is in savings accounts of one kind or another.
9. True
10. True
11. True
12. True
13. False because monetarists believe that velocity is predictable.
14. True
15. True
16. False because the precautionary motive for holding money says that people hold money in case of unexpected emergency needs.
17. False because as the interest rate falls, the demand for money increases because the opportunity cost of holding money falls.
18. True
19. False because the quantity of money demanded increases as the interest rate decreases.
20. False because MV = PQ.

Multiple Choice Questions

1. a	6. c	11. d	16. c
2. c	7. c	12. d	17. d
3. e	8. d	13. c	18. a
4. d	9. e	14. a	19. a
5. d	10. c	15. a	20. c

Problems

1. This situation reflects the paradox of thrift. By saving more, consumers cause national income to decline. The transactions demand for money falls, lowering the interest rate.

2. Follow the sequence of events: A decrease in the money supply will cause the interest rate to rise which will decrease investment spending which lowers aggregate expenditures and eliminates an inflationary gap. This is shown in the following graphs. A decrease in the money supply increases the interest rate to i' causing investment to decrease to I' and aggregate expenditures to decrease to AE" and the economy moves back to full employment.

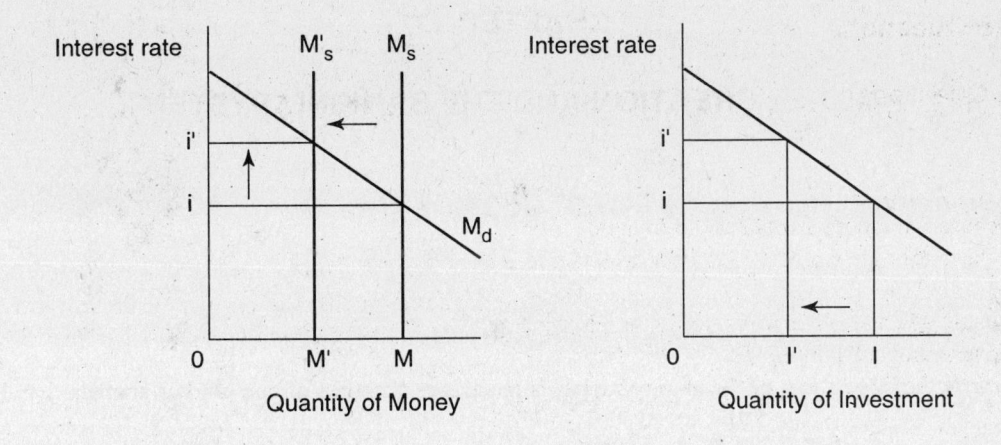

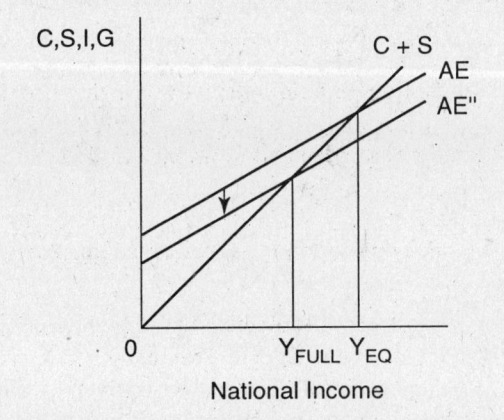

Discussion Questions

1. The response to this question is fairly obvious. Suppose your professor wanted a haircut. He or she would have to find a barber who wanted to listen to an economics lecture in payment for the haircut. The cost of finding such a barber might be very high indeed!

2. No, it doesn't because velocity is typically greater than one.

3. The equation of exchange—MV = PQ—merely shows that nominal GDP is equal to the money supply multiplied by the velocity of money. The quantity theory of money expresses a causal relationship: the price level is a function of the money supply.

4. A rise in the price level would cause the transactions demand for money to increase since nominal GDP rises. More money is required to purchase the aggregate supply at a higher price level. In the equation of exchange, a higher price level and a constant money supply requires that velocity increase in order for both sides of the equation to balance. Therefore, the expectation of higher inflation is associated with higher velocity.

CHAPTER 11

MONEY CREATION AND THE BANKING SYSTEM

Chapter Summary

The one fundamental idea that explains how banks create money is the *fractional reserve system*. Fractional reserve simply means that banks only have to keep on hand (in their vaults) a fraction of what people deposit in their banks, even though these people have the right to withdraw their deposits on demand (which is why their deposits are called demand deposits). How is this done? How can banks honor a promise to return deposits to people when their deposits aren't there? The answer is that people don't customarily ask for their deposits, certainly not all, and not all at one time. That's what banks count on and, for most of the time, it works.

What do banks do with the deposits, if they're not there? That's the "creation" story. When a bank receives a new deposit, it can loan out a portion of the deposit, leaving a fraction of the deposit on hand as reserves. How large that fraction held in reserves must be is determined by the Federal Reserve System (Fed). That's why they are called required reserves. When the borrower who took out the loan spends it on, say, building a house, the housebuilder now has the money and deposits it in his own bank. This second bank is now able to loan a portion of this new deposit, keeping on hand a fraction as required reserve. Its own loan provides income for someone else who deposits it in a third bank, and so on. The process repeats and the money supply expands.

The text shows this expansion in the form of a series of T-accounts where deposits show up as both the bank's liabilities (the bank owes the depositors) and its assets (it can used the deposit). Its assets can be held in many forms, including cash or loans.

Does this money creation process go on forever? Not really, because each round of deposit is less by the fraction held in reserve. Stretching it out, the new deposits eventually become close to zero. How much, then, does an initial deposit create in terms of total new deposits? The answer is given by the *potential money multiplier* which is 1/lrr, where lrr is the legal reserve requirement (in percentage terms).

The money supply is unlikely to expand to the extent indicated by the potential money multiplier for two reasons. First, banks may prefer to hold reserves in excess of those required. These are called excess reserves. Second, and more important, people may simply not borrow sufficiently to exhaust the full amount of the available reserves. In this case, excess reserves accumulate not because banks prefer to hold them but because nobody wants them. To the extent that excess reserves exist, the actual money multiplier will be lower than the potential money multiplier.

The money creation process can run in reverse gear. When someone withdraws a deposit, it means the bank's loans are more than its new and lower deposits can support. It must reduce its loans. But that creates its own round-after-round sequence of loan and deposit reductions. The undoing of loans and deposits can also result from the Fed's raising the reserve requirement. Now the bank is forced to convert loans to reserves, and the creation process works in reverse.

Banks sometimes fail when a large portion of the loans they made are not repaid. When people learn of someone else's bank failing, they become nervous about their own deposits and may choose to withdraw them. If many people behave this way, they may cause a "run on the bank." If an exceptionally large withdrawal take place in a short period of time, loans—many of which have been generating solid economic activity—must be called in, reducing the money supply and real GDP. The failure of a prominent bank alone can trigger waves of failures spreading to many banks, causing a dramatic decrease in the money supply. The Federal Deposit Insurance Corporation was created to ensure depositors' deposits—up to $100,000—so they would have less anxiety about the security of their deposits. Bank audits and examinations are also supposed to increase faith in the banking system by making certain that banks operate according to sound principles and legislated regulations.

However, in spite of FDIC and regular bank audits, banks do fail. During the 1980s and the early 1990s, bank failure rates rose significantly. A variety of causes account for these increased rates of bank failure. Savings and loans associations (S&Ls) also went through a difficult period during the 1980s as banks began to compete with them in the home mortgage market. Savings and loans failures were so extensive in the 1980s that a special government sponsored corporation, the Resolution Trust Corporation, had to be established in order to handle the claims of depositors and creditors of the failed S&Ls.

In the absence of intervention by a central bank, like the Fed, banking practice would tend to exacerbate the phases of the business cycle. During recession, a bank is less likely to lend for fear of not being repaid. The money supply shrinks as outstanding loans are called in, causing the interest rate to rise and investment to fall, just when investment is needed the most. During prosperity, banks are more inclined to lend, which causes the money supply to grow more rapidly than otherwise, resulting in lower interest rates and more borrowing. With the economy near or at full employment, it creates an upward pressure on the price level. The Fed can counteract these outcomes by using some of its monetary tools. That's what we examine in the next chapter.

Key Terms — Test your comprehension by defining and explaining the significance of these terms.

fractional reserve system
balance sheet
legal reserve requirement
financial intermediaries

potential money multiplier
excess reserves
Federal Deposit Insurance Corporation (FDIC)

True-False Questions — If a statement is false, explain why.

1. Banks keep all of their deposits on hand as reserves. (T/F)

2. The legal reserve requirement is the amount of capital that a bank must have in order to be chartered by the state. (T/F)

3. The legal reserve requirement is determined by the government. (T/F)

4. Banks may fail when an exceptionally large number of borrowers default on the loans they received from the bank, destroying, in this way, a large part of the bank's financial assets. (T/F)

5. One of the causes of the Savings and Loan crisis of the 1980s was the increased regulation of the banking industry. (T/F)

6. Increases in the legal reserve requirement increase the amount of money the banking system can create. (T/F)

7. Banks are eager to provide loans, thereby expanding the money supply during a recession. (T/F)

8. The cave illustration in the text shows how a fractional reserve system came into being. (T/F)

9. A demand deposit is the bank's asset; the loan it makes possible is the bank's liability. (T/F)

10. If a bank is allowed to lend $900 on a new deposit of $1,000, then the legal reserve requirement is 0.10. (T/F)

11. The potential money creation associated with a new deposit may be larger than the actual money creation because not all of the money that is made available for loans is actually loaned out. (T/F)

12. If the legal reserve requirement is 0.50, then a $100 deposit in the Paris First National Bank will allow the bank to create loans of $50. (T/F)

13. If the legal reserve requirement is 0.50, then a $100 deposit in the Paris First National Bank will allow the banking system to create $50 of new deposits. (T/F)

14. Excess reserves accumulate in a bank when the bank, intentionally or unintentionally, does not loan out the full potential of its assets, subject to the legal reserve requirement. (T/F)

15. FDIC insures all deposits in commercial banks up to their full amount. (T/F)

16. The number of bank failures in the 1980s exceeded the number of failed banks during the Great Depression years of the 1930s. (T/F)

17. Looking at a bank's balance sheet, its liabilities represent the failures of its borrowers to repay the banks loans. (T/F)

18. Regulation Q was a ceiling imposed on interest rates that banks and savings and loans were allowed to pay depositors. (T/F)

19. The principal role of financial intermediaries, such as banks, savings and loans associations, and credit unions is to accept deposits from savers and make loans to borrowers. (T/F)

20. Farmers who had borrowed heavily during the 1970s were squeezed during the 1980s as farm prices and land values fell. (T/F)

Multiple Choice Questions

1. A fractional reserve banking system is one in which banks within the system
   a. can lend out all of their reserves.
   b. keep on hand all of their reserves to honor depositors' needs for cash.
   c. can lend out only a fraction of their reserves.
   d. try to maximize their excess reserves.
   e. pay higher rates of interest to depositors than they charge borrowers to maximize deposits.

2. The potential money multiplier is equal to
   a. the income multiplier.
   b. the interest rate.
   c. one divided by the legal reserve requirement.
   d. the legal reserve requirement.
   e. one.

3. The amount of money created in the banking system by a new deposit may be less than the amount generated by multiplying the initial deposit by the potential money multiplier because
   a. many banks, intentionally or unintentionally, may end up holding excess reserves.
   b. many banks may end up with more liabilities than assets.
   c. many banks may end up with more assets than liabilities.
   d. the legal reserve requirements may be less than the requirements associated with the potential money multiplier.
   e. double counting of deposits may occur among banks in the system.

4. Prior to the 1980s, S&Ls were fairly stable financial institutions because
   a. they invested heavily in a buoyant stock market that produced relatively stable rates of return.
   b. they invested in high risk, high yielding bonds that earned higher than average rates of return.
   c. they were successful competing against commercial banks and credit unions for mortgage loans.
   d. they were able to open branches in more than one state, thereby diversifying their risks.
   e. they did not face competition from commercial banks in the home mortgage lending business.

5. Suppose you deposit $1,000 in a bank and the reserve requirement is 0.25. Suppose also that the banking system has zero excess reserves. The total amount of new money (not counting your deposit) created by the banking system is
   a. $3,000.
   b. $4,000.
   c. $1,000.
   d. $250.
   e. $750.

6. If the Federal Reserve raises the legal reserve requirement from 0.10 to 0.20, then
   a. banks will raise the interest rate to make up for the loss of their loan volumes.
   b. the potential money multiplier increases.
   c. banks will reduce the loans they make and the money supply in the economy will fall.
   d. banks will increase the loans they make and the money supply in the economy will rise.
   e. excess reserves will increase by 10 percent.

7. If the Federal Reserve sets the legal reserve requirement at 1.00, then
   a. banks could loan out as much money as they want.
   b. banks could loan out only the amount they hold in deposit.
   c. all bank deposits would be held as required reserves.
   d. the potential money multiplier would be infinite.
   e. each bank's liabilities would equal its assets.

8. When you deposit $100 in your local bank, even though you can withdraw that amount at any time
   a. the bank becomes the legal owner of that $100 deposit.
   b. it automatically and instantaneously creates $100 in the bank's reserves.
   c. the bank's assets become $100 more than its liabilities.
   d. the bank's balance sheet remains unchanged because its new asset equals its new liability.
   e. the potential money multiplier increases by $100 times the legal reserve requirement.

9. If you withdraw $100 from the bank the following month
   a. the bank's assets become $100 less than its liabilities.
   b. it automatically and instantaneously creates $100 in the bank's excess reserves.
   c. the potential money multiplier decreases by $100 times the legal reserve requirement.
   d. the money supply decreases.
   e. the money supply increases.

10. Assuming that every bank in the banking system holds substantial excess reserves, a decision by the Federal Reserve to increase the legal reserve requirement will
    a. cause the money supply to contract, but only slightly.
    b. cause the money supply to increase, but only slightly.
    c. force banks to decrease their excess reserves.
    d. create a wave of bank failures.
    e. cause the potential money multiplier to increase.

11. Bank runs most likely occur when
    a. depositors discover that other depositors were not able to withdraw their deposits from their own banks.
    b. borrowers who borrowed at high interest rates learn that interest rates are falling and will stay low for some time.
    c. banks are forced by government to become part of the FDIC.
    d. the Federal Reserve announces a series of upcoming bank audits.
    e. borrowers outnumber savers.

12. The Federal Deposit Insurance Corporation (FDIC) is designed to
    a. protect depositors from losing all their deposits in the event of bank failure.
    b. protect banks from being sued by depositors in the event of bank failure.
    c. protect banks against the possibility of bank failure.
    d. insure the deposits in the Federal Reserve System.
    e. safeguard the banking system against bank fraud.

13. Banks provided farmers during the 1970s with significant amounts of new debt because
    a. banks had considerable excess reserves they wished to divest.
    b. farmers were more willing than urban businesses to pay the high rates of interest banks demanded.
    c. prices of grain and land were rising, providing farmers with higher valued collateral to back the loans.
    d. government encouraged banks to make these loans in order to stabilize a sluggish farm economy.
    e. they knew that Willie Nelson would bail them out with Farm Aid.

14. Loans that U.S. bankers made to Mexico and Venezuela during the 1970s
    a. became very high-risk loans when the price of oil fell in the early 1980s.
    b. were quickly repaid in the 1980s, providing U.S. banks with considerable excess reserves.
    c. were at interest rates substantially higher than the U.S. rate which caused many Latin American projects to fail.
    d. were transformed by the Federal reserve to outright grants in the 1980s.
    e. were made at low rates of interest because of their commitment to fight poverty in Latin America.

15. Savings and loans associations, prior to the 1980s, were able to pay depositors relatively low rates of interest on their deposits because
    a. these rates were dictated by commercial banks.
    b. mortgage lending was relatively unprofitable for them.
    c. Regulation Q set ceilings on these rates.
    d. the S&Ls were monopolists.
    e. interest rates were falling dramatically in the early 1980s.

16. Contrary to what the economy really needs, the banking system tends to _____ during periods of recession and _____ during periods of prosperity.
    a. increase the money supply; decrease the money supply
    b. raise interest rates; lower interest rates
    c. decrease the money supply; increase the money supply
    d. increase its liabilities; decrease its assets
    e. decrease its liabilities; increase its assets

Discussion Questions

1. Suppose that I find $10,000 in a brown paper bag lying beside the Yellow Springs-Xenia bike path. I deposit this money in Star Bank in downtown Yellow Springs. Has the money supply increased? Why or why not?

2. Suppose that Star Bank in question 1 has a legal reserve requirement of 0.10. Can it make new loans as a result of my deposit assuming it had zero excess reserves prior to my deposit? Explain.

3. By how much can the money supply expand in the previous example? By how much will deposits expand? Why is there a difference?

4. Why is the potential money multiplier too large?

5. Why is the money supply too important to be left to the banks?

Answers to Questions

True-False Questions

1. False because banks only keep a fraction of their deposits on hand.
2. False because the legal reserve requirement is the fraction of deposits that must be kept as reserves.
3. False because the legal reserve requirement is determined by the Federal Reserve.
4. True
5. False because it followed the deregulation of the banking industry.
6. False because increases in the legal reserve requirement decrease the amount of money the banking system can create.
7. False because bankers will be reluctant to make loans during recession.
8. True
9. False because a demand deposit is a liability for a bank and a loan is an asset.
10. True
11. True
12. True
13. False because the banking system creates $400 in new money ($500, including the initial deposit).
14. True
15. False because FDIC only covers deposits up to $100,000.
16. True
17. False because the bank's liabilities are the deposits it holds.
18. True
19. True
20. True

Multiple Choice Questions

1. c	6. c	11. a	16. c
2. c	7. c	12. a	
3. a	8. b	13. c	
4. e	9. d	14. a	
5. a	10. a	15. c	

Discussion Questions

1. No, because this money was already part of M1.

2. Star Bank can make up to $9,000 in new loans.

3. Deposits can expand by $100,000 while the money supply can expand by $90,000. The difference is the initial deposit which adds to deposits but doesn't add to the money supply since it already was part of the money supply.

4. The potential money multiplier is too large because not all of excess reserves may be loaned and some of the money loaned will not find its way back into bank accounts.

5. Extreme fluctuations in the money supply can have a big impact on interest rates, investment, and the equilibrium level of national income. An unregulated banking system tends to foster an unstable economic environment when it causes the money supply to expand too rapidly during the prosperity phase of the business cycle and causes the money supply to contract too much during a downturn in the business cycle.

CHAPTER 12

THE FEDERAL RESERVE SYSTEM AND MONETARY POLICY

Chapter Summary

If necessity is the mother of invention, then the experiences of our early banking system cried out for the invention of central banking. Overindulging banks chronically overissued currency, kept too few reserves, and engaged in too high-risk loans, all of which undermined time and again the fragile, fledgling money economy. The Federal Reserve System came into existence in 1913 only after a history of failed attempts at central banking.

The money supply in 18th century colonial America consisted of a variety of foreign currencies and coins. A paper money—the Continentals, American money for the first time—was introduced during the revolutionary period only to be devalued quickly by massive overprinting. After independence, the number of state-chartered banks grew dramatically. Many feared—with justification—that these state banks would overissue currency and renew inflation. In order to counter this fear, the First Bank of the United States was established in 1791.

But it didn't last long. Opponents of the First Bank saw it as unconstitutional and a feared money monopoly. Congress refused to recharter. Soon after, the number of state banks and the amount of currency in circulation rose dramatically. Again, the money system was in trouble and a second try at central banking—the Second Bank of the United States—followed. Although widely regarded as having done a credible job, it too was unceremoniously discarded. Apart from the National Banking Acts during the Civil War, the history of banking in the United States from the 1830s to the eve of World War I was one of growing banking power over the economy but without control or direction.

The Panic of 1907 that followed the Knickerbocker Trust Disaster prompted United States political leaders to reconsider, once again, the need for a central bank. What emerged in 1913 was the Federal Reserve System (the Fed). The Fed is composed of twelve District Federal Reserve Banks, each owned by member banks that contribute three percent of their capital to the district bank. The main purpose of the Fed is to safeguard our money system. The Fed's Board of Governors consists of seven members appointed by the President for fourteen-year terms. The Chairman of the Board is a member who is appointed for a four-year term. District Federal Reserve Banks are also headed by boards of directors. The Federal Open Market Committee, one of the Fed's most important operating bodies, consists of twelve members, including seven from the Board of Governors, the President of the New York Fed, and four other district presidents who rotate. The Federal Open Market Committee controls the money supply via open market operations, the purchase and sale of government securities.

Have you ever wondered who prints our money? The Fed decides how much to print. The Fed also serves as a bankers' bank, keeping much of the commercial banks' reserves on deposit in its vaults, providing them with currency and loans, and clearing the billions of checks that travel cross-country through the banking system.

The Fed's principal goal is to manage the money supply. It has three operating tools at its disposal to achieve that goal. They are changing the legal reserve requirement, changing the discount rate, and engaging in open market operations. Suppose the Fed, worried about inflationary pressures in the economy, decides to decrease the money supply. What does it do? It can raise the legal reserve requirement which would force banks to hold a geater proportion of its deposits in reserve. In this way, banks lend out less, and the money supply decreases. Or it can raise the discount rate (the rate it charges member banks who borrow from the Fed) which makes banks' borrowing from the Fed less attractive. If they borrow less, the money supply decreases. Or the Fed may resort to its most effective and most frequently used monetary tool, that is, its open market operations. The Fed can sell government securities to the public, to members banks and to corporations, which draws money out of the banking system, thereby decreasing the money supply.

CHAPTER 12   THE FEDERAL RESERVE

These same instruments can be used to increase the money supply, although the effectiveness in this direction is somewhat weaker. The Fed can lower the legal reserve requirement, making more reserves available for loans. Note: it can make it available, but it can't make it happen. The Fed can lower the discount rate, but banks still have to want to borrow to make that policy work. The Fed's best move here is to buy government securities on the open market which will put more money in the hands of the securities' sellers. Still, they may deposit the money in their banks, but someone still has to want to borrow.

An alternative to controlling the money supply in order to manage the money economy, the Fed can choose to control the interest rate, allowing the money supply to take its course. It uses these same tools—reserve requirement, discount rate, and open market operations—to increase or decrease the interest rate.

A number of other tools—minor in comparison to the "big three"—are available to the Fed. Among these are stock market margin requirements and moral suasion. The Fed tends to be more effective at fighting inflation in high employment periods than it is at combatting unemployment during recessions. Ocassionally, the Fed and government pursue conflicting policies, one encouraging economic expansion while the other discourages it. Remember, the Fed is charged with managing the money economy and if it senses inflationary pressures mounting, it may curb economic activity even if it means creating unemployment. That's where the government steps in if it wants to protect jobs. It can use its fiscal policy to lower rates of unemployment at the same time the Fed uses its monetary policy to contain inflation. In this situation, they work at cross purposes. They did so through the mid-1980s when the Fed tended to maintain high interest rates while the government ran large, expansionary budget deficits.

Key Terms — Test your comprehension by defining and explaining the significance of these terms.

bank note
state-chartered bank
nationally chartered bank
Federal Reserve System (the Fed)
Federal Open Market Committee
discount rate

countercyclical monetary policy
reserve requirement
federal funds market
federal funds rate
open market operations
margin requirements

True-False Questions — If a statement is false, explain why.

1. Continental notes, issued by the Continental Congress to finance the American revolution, were paper money backed by gold. (T/F)

2. Alexander Hamilton was in favor of a central bank while the idea of a central bank was opposed by Jefferson and Madison. (T/F)

3. The Fed's primary goal, as mandated by Congress, is to promote full employment in the economy. (T/F)

4. The chief governing body of the Federal Reserve system is the Open Market Committee. (T/F)

5. Open market operations refer to the Fed's intervention in the stock market when it perceives that the market decline may endanger the stability of the economy. (T/F)

6. In the event that a bank, at the close of a banking day, discovers it is short of required reserves, it can borrow the needed reserves from its Federal Reserve District Bank, paying the discount rate. (T/F)

7. The biggest money problem faced in the United States from the late 18th century through the 19th century was the reluctance of banks to issue enough paper money. (T/F)

8. The most effective and frequently used tool the Fed has at its disposal to change the money supply is its open market operations. (T/F)

9. When the Fed sells a $100 government security to your local bank, the change in your bank's balance sheet occurs only in the composition of its assets; its liabilities remains unchanged. (T/F)

10. The Fed is often called the banker's bank because commercial banks can make deposits in, and can borrow from, it. (T/F)

11. District Federal Reserve banks play a vital role in clearing the millions of checks that are written daily by people and businesses. (T/F)

12. A newly elected President has the opportunity to appoint a new Chairman of the Federal Reserve Board of Governors and to replace the Board with new members. (T/F)

13. The Federal Open Market Committee can increase the money supply by buying government securities. (T/F)

14. The Federal Reserve System provides individuals and businesses with loans through the federal funds market, charging them the federal funds rate. (T/F)

15. The most commonly used tool the Fed has for changing the money supply is the legal reserve requirement. (T/F)

16. The discount rate, which is always lower than the federal funds rate, is the rate that commercial banks charge businesses. (T/F)

17. Commerical banks lend and borrow reserves among themselves in the federal funds market. (T/F)

18. Because the Fed does not know the exact position of the demand curve for money in the money market, it cannot target both the money supply and the interest rate at the same time. (T/F)

19. The Fed's countercyclical monetary policy is to decrease the money supply during recession because low-level GDP requires less money and to expand the money supply during prosperity because high-level GDP requires more money. (T/F)

20. Because the Fed gets its policy cues from government its monetary policy is always coordinated with the government's own fiscal policy. (T/F)

Multiple Choice Questions

1. When the First Bank of the United States, the U.S.'s first attempt at central banking, was established in 1791
   a. no other country had a central bank.
   b. the United States monetary system was plagued by the hoarding of bank notes.
   c. unanimous support for the bank was given by Congress.
   d. there were many other nationally chartered banks that served the functions of a central bank.
   e. there were already central banks functioning in England, Holland, and Sweden.

2. The National Banking Act of 1864, passed during the Civil War, legislated
   a. the establishment of an early version of the Fed.
   b. funds for the South to reconstruct.
   c. the creation of the Comptroller of the Currency.
   d. a significant increase in taxes to win the Civil War.
   e. greater competition in the banking industry.

3. If the Federal Open Market Committee decided to buy government securities on the open market, then we can expect
   a. an increase in the interest rate.
   b. an increase in the money supply.
   c. a decrease in the price level.
   d. a decrease in investment.
   e. the economy to approach full employment with zero inflation.

4. It is impossible for the Fed to target both the interest rate and the money supply simultaneously because
   a. the money supply is hard to calculate precisely.
   b. the Fed can't control money demand.
   c. the interest rate is determined on the money market, not by the Fed.
   d. Congress has veto power over the Fed's decision-making process.
   e. this would be unconstitutional.

5. One of the problems the Fed faces using its monetary policy to expand aggregate demand during a recession is
   a. banks may be reluctant to make loans and businesses may be reluctant to borrow from banks.
   b. the government may be using its fiscal policy to decrease aggregate demand.
   c. expanding aggregate demand only leads to inflation.
   d. the aggregate supply curve would shift to the right, creating more unemployment.
   e. workers will be unwilling to accept lower wage rates which will occur if aggregate demand expands.

6. All of the following are mechanisms the Fed can use to increase the money supply except
   a. selling securities on the open market.
   b. buying securities on the open market.
   c. lowering the reserve requirement.
   d. lowering the discount rate.
   e. lowering the margin requirement on loans to purchase stocks.

7. The Federal Reserve Act of 1913 created the Federal Reserve System, not the Federal Reserve Bank, because
   a. the U.S. already had experience with a central bank, and it didn't work.
   b. the government wanted to keep the entire money system, not just the banks, under its control.
   c. Congress wanted a decentralized central bank.
   d. state-chartered and nationally chartered banks were already operating in the economy.
   e. the government planned to link the central bank to the Department of the Treasury.

8. The discount rate is determined by
   a. supply and demand in the money market.
   b. supply and demand in the federal funds market.
   c. nationally chartered banks, although it applies as well to state-chartered banks
   d. the Fed.
   e. the Department of the Treasury.

9. Monetary policy is more effective curbing inflation than reducing unemployment because during periods of high unemployment
   a. banks are more reluctant to lend to businesses and businesses are more reluctant to borrow.
   b. businesses may wish to borrow, but banks are reluctant to lend.
   c. the Fed can rely on the self-correcting behavior of the labor market.
   d. providing easier credit never stimulates borrowing.
   e. the government will act, making the Fed's participation unnecessary and even interfering.

10. When the government tries to finance a deficit by issuing new government securities while, at the same time, the Fed pursues policies to encourage more borrowing by businesses
    a. the government and the Fed should raise the interest rate.
    b. the Fed should buy the government's new securities issues.
    c. government's policy and the Fed's policy have opposite effects on the interest rate.
    d. the new govenent securities issues will lower the interest rate which is what the Fed wants anyway.
    e. the Fed should lower the interest rate which will allow the government to sell the new securities more easily.

11. During recession, an appropriate pair of policies for the Fed to implement would be to
    a. lower the discount rate and purchase government securities.
    b. increase the discount rate and purchase government securities.
    c. raise the legal reserve requirement and lower the discount rate.
    d. sell government securities and raise the discount rate.
    e. raise the discount rate and lower the legal reserve requirement.

12. Moral suasion and controlling stock market margin requirements are two of the
    a. strongest tools used by the Fed to control the money supply.
    b. ancillary tools used by the Fed to control the money supply.
    c. quite effective at fine-tuning monetary policy.
    d. tools only used to decrease the money supply.
    e. tools only used to increase the money supply.

13. When the Fed raises the legal reserve requirement
    a. it forces banks to call in loans and convert them to reserves.
    b. it decreases the amount of reserves banks are obligated to hold.
    c. it creates the conditions for bank loan expansion.
    d. it makes government securities more attractive because interest rates fall.
    e. it lowers the discount rate that the Fed charges commercial banks.

14. When the Fed buys government securities in the open market, the effect on the asset positions of commercial banks is
    a. negative, forcing banks to call in loans and converting them to reserves.
    b. positive, decreasing the amount of reserves banks are obligated to hold.
    c. an increase in bank reserves which allow banks to increase lending.
    d. a substitution of stocks and corporate bonds for government securities.
    e. to increase banks' assets, but at the same time, their liabilities.

15. The most likely place for a commercial bank to go to increase its reserves for short periods is
    a. its district Federal Reserve bank.
    b. the federal open market committee.
    c. the federal funds market.
    d. the Department of the Treasury.
    e. Knickerbocker Trust.

16. All of the following are roles played by the Fed as a bankers' bank except
    a. clearing checks.
    b. providing currency.
    c. providing loans.
    d. providing customers for commercial loans.
    e. holding the reserves of member banks.

17. The main role of the Federal Reserve System is to safeguard the country's money system by
    a. controlling the money supply, interest rates, and the price level.
    b. doing thorough monthly audits of all nationally chartered banks.
    c. encouraging District Feds to monitor all business transactions generated in their districts that exceed $1,000,000.
    d. putting in place monetary policy that helps Congress cut the deficit.
    e. keeping very conservative bankers on the Board of Governors.

18. U.S. Bureau of Printing and Engraving in Washington, D.C. prints our currency
    a. but the Department of the Treasury determines when and how much should be introduced into the economy.
    b. and determines how much of it should be introduced into the economy.
    c. but District Federal Reserve Banks determine when and how much should be introduced into the economy.
    d. but the Federal Open Market Committee determines when and how much should be introduced into the economy.
    e. but the government, through fiscal policy, determines when and how much should be introduced into the economy.

19. There are _____ District Federal Reserve Banks in the United States.
    a. 6
    b. 10
    c. 12
    d. 15
    e. 50

20. The Fed's use of moral suasion to control inflation
    a. is very effective because people know the alternative to moral suasion is strong government fiscal policy.
    b. is always tried before the Fed resorts to other tools of monetary policy.
    c. is inherently weak because it relies on voluntary compliance.
    d. is preferred by banks because it is more convenient than having to pay the higher discount rates at the Fed.
    e. is only used in combination with the Fed's other tools of monetary policy.

Discussion Questions

1. How stable were financial institutions in the United States prior to the establishment of the Federal Reserve System? Provide examples.

2. Why is monetary policy a more effective tool for controlling inflation than for controlling unemployment?

3. Outline the institutional structure of the Federal Reserve System. Why are there twelve District Banks in the Fed instead of one central bank?

4. Describe the tools used by the Fed to manipulate the money supply and interest rates.

5. When might the Fed use a money supply target? When would it probably employ an interest rate target? Why?

CHAPTER 12   THE FEDERAL RESERVE   MONEY, BANKING, AND MONETARY POLICY   119

Answers to Questions

True-False Questions

1. False because they were not backed by gold.
2. True
3. False because the country banks would then withdraw their deposits in the spring creating instability in the banking system.
4. False because the chief governing body is the Board of Governors.
5. False because open market operations are purchases and sales of government securities by the Fed.
6. True
7. False because the biggest problem was issuing too much currency.
8. True
9. True
10. True
11. True
12. False because the terms of the Chairman and the Board extend over more than one political administration.
13. True
14. False because the Federal Reserve notes are issued by the District Feds.
15. False because the most commonly used tool is the open market operations.
16. False because banks borrow from each other at the federal funds rate.
17. True
18. True
19. False because a countercyclical policy would increase the money supply during a downturn and decrease the money supply during a period of inflation.
20. True

Multiple Choice Questions

1. e	6. a	11. a	16. d
2. c	7. c	12. b	17. a
3. b	8. d	13. a	18. c
4. b	9. a	14. c	19. c
5. a	10. c	15. c	20. c

Discussion Questions

1. The banking system was chronically unstable. Among the notable examples are the large numbers of bank failures in 1815–1816 prior to the establishment of the Second Bank of the United States and the Knickerbocker Trust crisis in 1907. The problem that a central bank might have helped to solve was the tendency of banks to issue more currency than their reserves could support. Bank failures would occur in waves with no mechanism for stopping the withdrawal of deposits from the nation's banks. A central bank could have provided liquidity to banks under pressure from depositors making withdrawals during periods of economic and financial uncertainty.

2. The Fed would want to increase aggregate demand in order to reduce unemployment and, while the Fed can make loans available to banks in the expectation that it would increase bank lending and economic activity, it can't force the banks to borrow from the Fed nor can the banks force businesses to borrow for investment. On the other hand, during inflation, the Fed can increase interest rates by making loans less available to banks and in doing so make borrowing more expensive, which will decrease aggregate demand and consequently relax the upward pressure on the price level.

3. The Fed is controlled by a seven member board with one member appointed as the Chair. The board members have 14-year terms and the Chair serves for four years with the potential for reappointments for up to 14 years. The Fed Open Market Committee consists of the Board and five of the District Fed Presidents, one of whom must be the New York Fed President. District Fed Presidents rotate on and off the Open Market Committee. Open market operations are the purchase and sale of government securities by the Fed. There are 12 District Feds to better serve the regions of the United States and to diffuse power throughout the Federal Reserve system.

4. The Fed can change the legal reserve requirement, change the discount rate, use open market operations, change the stock market margin requirement, and use moral suasion to alter the money supply and interest rates.

5. The Fed is most inclined to use a money supply target when inflation is a serious problem. By restricting the money supply, the price level should fall. An interest rate target is preferred to fight unemployment since, by lowering interest rates, aggregate demand can be stimulated.

CHAPTER 13

CAN GOVERNMENT REALLY STABILIZE THE ECONOMY?

Chapter Summary

There is little consensus among economists on macroeconomic policy not only because they have imperfect information to work with but because they approach economic issues from very different political perspectives. It is not altogether surprising, then, that liberal economists tend to be more inclined to advocate government intervention in the economy than do conservative economists. The fact that our presidents typically choose economic advisors who share their political ideologies is also hardly surprising.

Macroeconomic theorists, who represent a wide range of ideologies, have focused most of their attention on why unemployment and inflation exist and what can be done about them. Different schools of thought—classical, Keynesian, neo-Keynesian, rational expectations, and supply-side economics—reflecting differences in ideology have developed around the issues of unemployment, inflation, and policies to prevent them. Even within schools of thought there are significant divergences of opinion.

The classical school believes that unemployment is no more than a temporary phenomenon. They believe that markets are competitive so that prices are flexible and always moving toward equilibrium where quantity demanded equals quantity supplied. Under these circumstances, labor markets—given enough time—will always generate full employment. The appropriate policy for dealing with unemployment, then, is to not intervene. To classical economists, inflation is purely the result of too much money in circulation. The rate of growth of the money supply should match the rate of growth of real GDP so that prices remain stable. The quantity theory of money shows the relationship between the money supply and the price level. The Fed's intervention in the money system, as the classical school sees it, ends up being a cure worse than the disease.

Keynesian economists see the world very differently. They argue that prices are rigid and markets are not competitive. A decrease in demand leads to a decrease in output rather than a decrease in price. Under these circumstances, unemployment can persist indefinitely if nothing is done to prevent it. Increases in government spending, decreases in taxes, and increases in the money supply are all appropriate policies for combatting unemployment according to Keynesians. As long as the economy is at or below full employment, inflation poses no problems for Keynesians.

To the Keynesians' dismay, the 1970s and 1980s generated both high rates of unemployment and high rates of inflation. The term stagflation was coined to describe this unhappy coincidence. If the policy to cure unemployment was exactly the opposite of what their policy was to cure inflation, how do they cure both at the same time? Many Keynesians conceded that it just couldn't be done. Then what? Enter the Phillips curve. It was used to explain how higher rates of inflation could be traded for lower rates of unemployment. That is to say, as unemployment decreases, inflation increases. Neo-Keynesians developed a new version of the aggregate supply curve (Keynesian version representing the old) with an upward-sloping segment depicting price level increases as full employment is approached.

Neo-Keynesians developed new stabilization policy that worked off the Phillips curve. Suppose the government wants to lower the rate of unemployment. It increases its spending (that's what Keynesians would do), which raises GDP and employment. But that's only the beginning of the story. Workers now feel more comfortable to press for higher wages, which creates cost-push inflation (that's not what Keynesians expected). In other words, the government has to make a choice between accepting unemployment or inflation, or some combination of both. That's still not the end of the story. Neo-Keynesian economists pushed the analysis further, with more devastating results. When cost-push inflation occurs because of the initial government spending to lower unemployment, workers discover their real wages eroding and react by demanding wage increases to make up for the loss. If successful, these wage increases cut into firms' profit, discouraging production so that GDP falls and unemployment increases. Neo-Keynesians now conclude that while government can lower unemployment rates in the short run, it is much less successful in keeping them low in the long run.

Rational expectations theorists deny even these temporary short-run gains. They argue that the trade-off between unemployment and inflation suggested by the Phillips curve does not exist. Why? Because workers are rational and can translate past experience into expectations about the future. Let's go back to the first announcement by government that it will increase spending to lower the rate of unemployment. Workers expect such a policy to create inflation and, before suffering the expected real wage erosion, demand wage increases to compensate for the expected inflation. Their success undermines the government's employment policy because firms, paying the higher wages, have no incentive to increase production. The unemployment rate doesn't fall. According to rational expectations theorists, the government can't lower unemployment rates even in the short run and if it tries, succeeds only in raising the rate of inflation.

Supply-side economists argue that the best way to attack the problem of unemployment and inflation is by implementing policies that will move the aggregate supply curve to the right more rapidly over time. Such policies include lower tax rates, less government regulation, and less government spending. Policies that are good for the business environment are good supply-side policies. Supply-siders, in their criticisms of demand-side Keynesian policy, emphasize the crowding-out effect of fiscal policy. To finance its spending and deficits, government resorts to selling its own securities (savings bonds, for example) on the securities market, which competes directly with private firms who try to sell their own securities to finance private investment. In this way, government spending crowds out private investment.

Stabilization policy is described as discretionary, meaning that policy is a matter of judgment. But not all stabilization policy relies on judgment. To some extent, the economy can stabilize itself automatically. Unemployment insurance is one type of automatic stabilizer. During a recession, when unemployment increases, unemployment insurance payments increase and prop up aggregate demand somewhat. At full employment, these payments are lower, thus relieving inflationary pressure. The income and corporate profits taxes work similarly. During periods of high unemployment, the total of tax receipts is lower, with progressivity allowing people to keep a larger percentage of their earnings. When the economy is at full employment, tax revenues rise and, as people move into higher tax brackets, they are able to spend smaller percentages of their total earnings which relieves some inflationary pressure. If these automatic stabilizers are effective, then the need for active government intervention to stabilize the economy diminishes.

Key Terms — Test your comprehension by defining and explaining the significance of these terms.

classical economics
stabilization policy
Keyensian economics
Phillips curve
neo-Keynesian economics

rational expectations
supply-side economics
crowding out
automatic stabilizers

True-False Questions — If a statement is false, explain why.

1. The different views held by economists regarding proper economic policy may reflect their political ideologies as much as their understanding of how the economy works. (T/F)

2. A primary assumption underlying the classical school's view of the economy is that firms are highly competitive. (T/F)

3. The Keynesian idea of fine-tuning the economy rests on the belief that it is possible through fiscal and monetary policies to lower rates of unemployment and rates of inflation simultaneously. (T/F)

4. The Phillips curve represents combinations of rates of unemployment and rates of inflation that are directly related. (T/F)

5. The long-run Phillips curve model of the Neo-Keynesian school suggests that monetary and fiscal policy can achieve only temporary victories in lowering the rate of unemployment. (T/F)

6. Fiscal policy to reduce high rates of unemployment is especially effective if the long-run Phillips Curve is vertical. (T/F)

7. A beneficial effect of lowering the deficit is that government borrowing may decline which should cause interest rates to decline as well. (T/F)

8. One advantage associated with automatic stabilizers is that no decision making is necessary for them to work. (T/F)

9. The classical school explains unemployment in the economy as the result of interference from unions and minimum wage laws in labor markets. (T/F)

10. A classical school economist would agree with a Keynesian that the cause of inflation is most often excessive aggregate demand. (T/F)

11. According to classical economists, if the economy is at full employment and velocity is constant, then an appropriate rate of growth for the money supply is precisely the rate of growth of real GDP. (T/F)

12. The idea that anticipation of fiscal policy by consumers and producers and their reacting to it before it occurs is the centerpiece of the rational expectations school. (T/F)

13. Keynesians view inflation as a serious economic problem. (T/F)

14. During the high inflation years of the Nixon presidency, wage and price controls were applied which permanently altered the Phillips curve combinations of rates of unemployment and inflation in the economy. (T/F)

15. The upward-sloping segment of the aggregate supply curve reflects the inverse relationship between rates of unemployment and rates of inflation shown in the Phillips curve. (T/F)

16. Raising tax rates to curb inflation is a cornerstone of supply-side economics. (T/F)

17. Supply-side economists argue that supply shocks to the economy, such as the OPEC-engineered increase in oil prices, could be avoided if the government pursues vigorous fiscal policy. (T/F)

18. If workers are successful in bargaining for wage increases to offset the increase in inflation associated with government policies to combat unemployment, then the long-run Phillips curve will be vertical. (T/F)

19. A rational expectations theorist believes that it is possible to lower the unemployment rate, but only temporarily. (T/F)

20. The Laffer curve suggests that a cut in the tax rate can actually increase tax revenues. (T/F)

Multiple Choice Questions

1. When asked "What causes inflation," a classical economist's most probable answer would be
   a. excessive growth in the money supply.
   b. tight monetary policy on the part of the Fed.
   c. a supply shock.
   d. excessive growth in aggregate demand.
   e. the lack of an effective program of wage-price controls.

2. In a world characterized by rational expectations, a Fed announcement that they intend to lower interest rates is likely to result in
   a. a run on banks.
   b. unions and other workers bargaining for a wage increase.
   c. a decrease in the price level.
   d. a decrease in unemployment.
   e. a shift in the Phillips curve to the left.

3. Supply-side economists argue that policies favoring businesspeople will
   a. shift the aggregate supply curve to the right.
   b. cause the deficit to increase.
   c. cause aggregate demand to increase more rapidly than aggregate supply.
   d. lower inflation but not unemployment.
   e. create labor unrest among workers.

4. All of the following are sources of inflation according to a neo-Keynesian economist except
   a. the influence of unions.
   b. a hike in oil prices.
   c. crop failures throughout much of the world.
   d. the money supply growing at the same rate as real GDP.
   e. market power wielded by monopolists and oligopolists.

5. Classical economists believe that the economy will automatically adjust to full employment because
   a. aggregate demand will increase, causing real GDP and employment to increase.
   b. aggregate supply will decrease, causing inflation to fall and employment to increase.
   c. the economy is highly competitive.
   d. union membership will increase so that its market power will be effective in creating more employment.
   e. employers will raise wages to keep its workers so that real GDP and employment will increase.

6. The main difference between Keynesians and neo-Keynesians is that Keynesians believe it is possible to eliminate unemployment _____ and neo-Keynesians believed that in the battle over unemployment _____.
   a. permanently with zero inflation; only temporary victories with some inflation are possible
   b. only temporary victories with some inflation are possible; permanently with zero inflation
   c. permanently with some inflation; only temporary victories are possible but with no inflation
   d. with great difficulty because of structural unemployment; structural unemployment is of little concern
   e. without government intervention; government intervention is necessary

7. An essential component of the rational expectations model is that
   a. wages are rigid, at least when aggregate demand falls.
   b. unions leaders can be made to see why stabilizing wages stabilizes prices.
   c. unions are not very powerful.
   d. wages are quite flexible.
   e. monetary policy is totally ineffective.

8. All of the following would be consistent with supply-side policies except
   a. a cut in income taxes.
   b. cuts in subsidies for research and development.
   c. cuts in corporate profits taxes.
   d. tax credits for firms that pursue research and development.
   e. a hike in capital gains taxes.

9. The Humphrey-Hawkins Act of 1978
   a. called on government to pursue zero unemployment and zero inflation policies.
   b. acknowledged the impossibility of pursuing zero unemployment and zero inflation.
   c. put rational expectations policies into effect.
   d. forced unions to accept lower wage rate increases to keep unemployment rates low.
   e. created wage and price controls to control both inflation and unemployment.

10. All of the following are characteristics of the classical model of the economy except
    a. flexible wages.
    b. monopoly power.
    c. increases in the price level that are proportionate to increases in the money supply.
    d. competitive markets.
    e. flexible prices.

11. A Keynesian would view inflation as an unlikely chronic problem because
    a. the aggregate supply curve is horizontal until full employment is reached.
    b. central banks monitor the money supply.
    c. real GDP growth will eliminate any inflationary pressure from building in the economy.
    d. technology shifts the aggregate supply curve to the left, raising real GDP and lowering inflation.
    e. the long-run Phillips Curve is vertical.

12. The neo-Keynesian view of the Phillips curve is that the curve
    a. shifts upward over time because government keeps trying to lower the rate of unemployment.
    b. is constant, although government policy may shift the economy's position on the curve.
    c. shows no correlation between rates ot unemployment and rates of inflation.
    d. is vertical in the short run, but becomes less steep in the long run.
    e. is horizontal so unemployment can be reduced to low levels without causing inflation.

13. According to rational expectations theorists, the main effect of an expansionary fiscal or monetary policy is to
    a. lower the level of unemployment at the cost of somewhat higher inflation.
    b. create a shift to the right in the aggregate supply curve.
    c. cause workers to bargain for a wage increase in advance of an increase in the price level, causing inflation.
    d. raise the rates of both autonomous and induced investment.
    e. create a larger pool of savings from which investors can borrow.

14. The most appropriate stabilization policy, according to the classical school, is to
    a. do nothing.
    b. rely on monetary policy, not fiscal policy, in order to keep government interference minimal.
    c. rely on aggressive fiscal policy immediately when problems arise to keep the problem from expanding.
    d. make sure the Phillips curve does not shift in either direction.
    e. apply wage and price controls to stabilize employment and inflation.

15. An example of an automatic stabilizer is
    a. fiscal policy.
    b. the Laffer curve.
    c. the Phillips curve.
    d. the Full Employment Act of 1946.
    e. unemployment insurance.

16. Wage and price controls were advocated by neo-Keynesians in an attempt to
    a. prevent monopolies from raising prices even when the economy is at low levels of employment.
    b. reduce government's control over the economy.
    c. avoid market instabilities.
    d. prevent wage and price increases from undermining the cuts in unemployment resulting from government policy.
    e. prevent unions from extending their control to all workers in the economy.

17. The school most closely associated with the idea that government can stabilize the economy is
    a. Keynesian.
    b. classical.
    c. neo-Keynesian.
    d. rational expectation.
    e. supply-side.

18. The Full Employment Act of 1946 made it government policy to insure that
    a. real wages rise steadily over time.
    b. there will be employment for all those willing and able to work.
    c. deficit spending be used to increase aggregate demand.
    d. unions represent workers who lose their jobs.
    e. Keynesian economists be consulted before government makes economic policy decisions.

19. One of the reasons why the coexistence of inflation and unemployment of the late 1960s and 1970s was a surprise to Keynesian economists was that
    a. Keynesians didn't think inflation would arise with high unemployment rates.
    b. Keynesians didn't think inflation was possible in a modern economy.
    c. fiscal policies to increase aggregate demand are naturally anti-inflationary.
    d. inflation could be stopped successfully with wage-price controls.
    e. inflation was viewed as only a temporary phenomenon with wages and prices adjusting back downward automatically once full employment was reached.

20. The progressive income tax is an example of an automatic stabilizer because
    a. when GDP increases, tax revenues increase at a faster rate, reducing the upward pressure on prices.
    b. the progressive income tax is a permanent structure in our economy.
    c. people automatically pay their taxes on April 15th, regardless of whether GDP increases or decreases.
    d. people tend to forget their tax obligations when they consume so that aggregate demand is always high.
    e. people use some of their savings to pay for taxes.

Discussion Questions

1. Compare and contrast the Keynesian and classical models of the economy. Use graphs in your analysis.

2. Sketch the Phillips Curve diagram and explain the logic behind the relationship between inflation and unemployment that is represented.

3. Why is the long-run Phillips Curve vertical?

4. How well do expansionary fiscal and monetary policies work in a world of rational expectations? What about contractionary policies? Explain.

5. Give some examples of supply-side policies. Critique the argument that supply-side economists make about the impact of their policies on the economy.

6. What is meant by the term *crowding out*? How could crowding out act as a drag on economic growth over time?

CHAPTER 13 CAN GOV'T STABILIZE THE ECONOMY?

Answers to Questions

True-False Questions

1. True
2. True
3. True
4. False because rates of unemployment and inflations are inversely related.
5. True
6. False because no policy would be effective if the long-run Phillips curve is vertical.
7. True
8. True
9. True
10. False because classical economists associate inflation with excessive growth in the money supply.
11. True
12. True
13. False because Keynesians believe that the economy tends to operate below full employment where inflation is not a serious problem.
14. False because inflation reappeared once the wage and price controls were lifted.
15. True
16. False because supply-side economists advocate lower tax rates.
17. False because supply-side economists advocate less government spending in the economy.
18. True
19. False because a rational expectations theorist believes that attempts to lower the unemployment rate are futile.
20. True

Multiple Choice Questions

1. a	6. a	11. a	16. d
2. b	7. d	12. a	17. a
3. a	8. e	13. c	18. b
4. d	9. b	14. a	19. a
5. c	10. b	15. e	20. a

Discussion Questions

1. The Keynesian and classical views can be compared using the following graphs. The left panel, depicting the classical view, shows a labor market in which wages are flexible. As demand for labor falls from D to D' the wage rate falls from $10 to $6. Note that at the $6 wage rate everyone willing to work for $6 has a job. That's what the supply curve for labor shows and that describes full employment. In the Keynesian case, a fall in demand for a good from D to D' causes output and employment to decrease. That's unemployment and as long as price remains inflexible at $10, the unemployment persists.

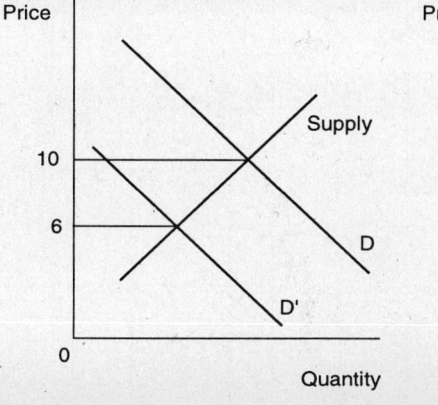

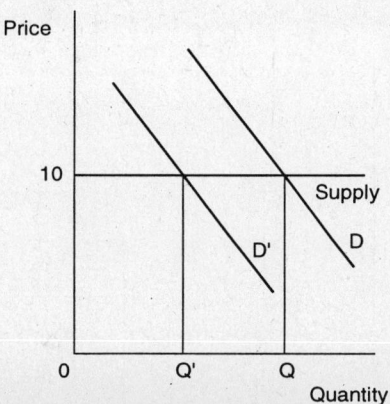

2. The Phillips curve shows the inverse relationship between rates of unemployment on the horizontal axis and rates of inflation on the vertical axis. As the economy approaches full employment, upward pressure on wages and prices causes inflation to rise, and vice-versa.

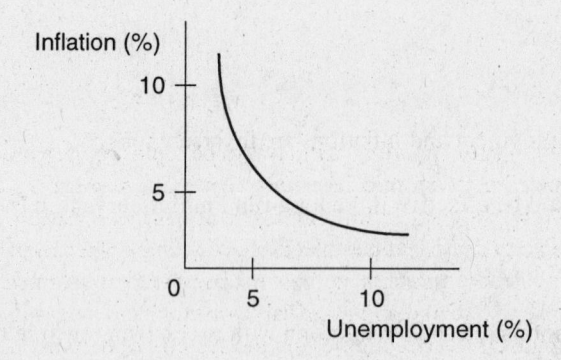

3. Suppose the government wants to lower the rate of unemployment. It increases its spending, which raises GDP and employment. Unions now feel more comfortable to press for higher wages which creates cost-push inflation. Workers and unions now discover their real wages eroding and react by demanding wage increases to make up for the loss. If successful, these wage increases cut into firms' profit, discouraging production so that GDP falls and unemployment increases. In other words, while government can lower unemployment rates in the short run, it is much less successful in keeping them low in the long run. If government keeps trying to lower unemployment rates, they only succeed in raising the rate of inflation. On the graph, it maps out a vertical Phillips curve.

4. Expansionary fiscal and monetary policies don't work at all because workers anticipate the increase in inflation they will cause and bargain for wage increases in advance preventing the policy from having any effect other than to increase the price level. Contractionary policies to cut aggregate demand to fight inflation work well. Workers immediately accept wage cuts in anticipation of a lower price level so the unemployment rate does not increase as aggregate demand falls.

5. Tax cuts are at the heart of supply-side policies. They advocate less government spending amd less government regulation. The intent is to move the aggregate supply curve to the right more rapidly over time.

6. Crowding out is the idea that government finance of deficit spending by borrowing pushes up interest rates and causes private investment to be crowded out of the economy in a manner that will slow down the accumulation of capital and create a lower rate of economic growth over time.

CHAPTER 14

GOVERNMENT SPENDING

Chapter Summary

The level and composition of government spending will always be topics for debate. Decisions about government spending are value judgments as well as economic decisions. Government spending is more than an instrument of fiscal policy. Even if the economy was always at full employment without inflation, there would still be a role for government. After all, we do need city streets, interstates, schools, environmental protection, and national defense. These goods are not typically provided by markets, at least not in sufficient quantities. Economists call them public goods because they are basically nonexclusive and nonrival. Nonexclusive means that no one can be excluded from consuming the good—like walking a city street or enjoying the security of national defense—and nonrival means that any person's consumption of that good does not diminish the good for other people—like walking that street doesn't lessen anybody else's use of that street. By contrast, umbrellas are not public goods because the owner can exclude others from using it, and when one uses it, it is not available to someone else at the same time.

Aside from its stablization and public goods provider roles, the government also legislates and administers transfer payments. Transfer payments are payments by government to particular groups in society. These are in the form of price subsidies, payment of goods-in-kind, or direct cash payments. Approximately 55 percent of federal spending is on transfer payments and only 31 percent is for provision of public goods. By contrast, 80 percent of state and local government spending is for the purchase of public goods.

The chapter describes federal, state and local spending item by item. Security is an important spending item. Most federal spending on security is for national defense. State and local spending is split between police and corrections. Federal spending on security has been falling as a percentage of GDP since the period after World War II.

There has always been strong support for public schools. By the second half of the nineteenth century, states were taxing to support both high schools and public universities. Spending on education has ranged from about 4 to 5.5 percent of GDP in the period since 1960.

Transportation, natural resources, energy, and space are all areas receiving government support. These areas exhibit the characteristics of public goods, though to varying degrees. In each area, competing groups press for different levels of spending. Though the debate over the appropriate level of spending in these areas is fierce, each has its own history and reasons for existence.

Spending programs for agriculture and public assistance are more people-specific than spending on defense, education, or transportation. Agriculture receives public money because it is felt that farm incomes might suffer significantly otherwise, jeopardizing the health of regional economies. Public assistance shows up as spending on housing, Medicaid, Aid to Families with Dependent Children, Supplemental Security Income, and food stamps. Public assistance as a percentage of total spending by government has grown from 2.9 percent in 1960 to 11 percent in 1990.

Since the 1930s, government has taken on the job of providing social insurance. The best known of these insurance programs is Social Security. Social Security is a compulsory program that transfers income across income and age groups. Low wage earners tend to receive more benefits relative to their contributions than do high wage earners. Younger workers paying Social Security taxes subsidize people in retirement who receive benefits. Unemployment insurance is another type of government social insurance program. Medicare provides health insurance for the elderly. Social insurance payments have risen dramatically from $42.3 billion in 1960 to $219.5 billion in 1990, measured in constant dollars. Still, Social Security transfer payments in the United States are somewhat below average for OECD countries.

Interest payments on the government debt are a growing percentage of federal spending, rising from about 7 percent in the 1960s and 1970s to 14 percent by 1990. Simply administering the affairs of government requires a considerable sum of money. Government spending has increased from about 28 percent of GDP in 1960 to some 36 percent of GDP in 1990. According to the Peacock-Wiseman hypothesis, government spending tends to rise most rapidly in periods of emergency like wars and depressions and then stay at these new, higher levels. Their hypothesis seems to hold for other OECD countries too, where levels of government spending are following the same trends as in the United States but are generally higher as percentages of GDP. As a share of GDP, federal, state, and local purchases of GDP amounted to about 19 percent in 1990. To the extent that government spending moves resources away from the provision of private goods to the provision of public goods, resource allocation is affected. Over time, a rising share of our resources have been devoted to the provision of public goods.

Key Terms — Test your comprehension by defining and explaining the significance of these terms.

Medicaid
Aid to Families with Dependent Children
Supplemental Security Income (SSI)
food stamp program
Social Security (OASDI)
unemployment insurance
Medicare

True-False Questions — If a statement is false, explain why.

1. Government spending on goods and services is strictly an economic decision. (T/F)

2. Your consumption of a public good does not exclude others from consuming it as well. (T/F)

3. The nonrival characteristic of a public good means your consuming it does not lessen the utility others can derive from it. (T/F)

4. If there was no government, there would be no public goods available because the market would not produce them. (T/F)

5. Social Security doesn't really help those in retirement because they had to pay for what they receive earlier in their careers. (T/F)

6. Although the government pays interest on the public debt, it is a small and declining part of federal spending. (T/F)

7. The largest share of federal government spending is on transfer payments. (T/F)

8. National defense spending represents the fastest growing item in the federal budget. (T/F)

9. The space program represents the most recent addition to the federal government's transfer payments program. (T/F)

10. The federal government's farm program represents transfer payments (from nonfarmers) to farmers. (T/F)

11. Food stamps can be legally converted to cash at most grocery stores. (T/F)

12. Medicare is available to those over 65 years old while Medicaid is a health care program for the poor. (T/F)

13. Social Security benefits only go to those who are over 65 years old. (T/F)

14. Adjusted for inflation, social insurance payments have increased more rapidly than real GDP from 1960 to 1990. (T/F)

15. As a percent of GDP, government spending in the U.S. is less than government spending in West European economies. (T/F)

16. The Peacock-Wiseman hypothesis suggests that government spending rises during crises but falls rapidly back to its original levels after the crises end. (T/F)

17. A legitimate argument for cutting government spending is that the private market will provide sufficient amounts of the sorts of goods and services that government provides and do it more efficiently. (T/F)

Multiple Choice Questions

1. Government spends to provide all of the following except
    a. public goods.
    b. transfer payments.
    c. countercyclical fiscal policy.
    d. countercyclical monetary policy.
    e. administration of government institutions.

2. To say that a good is nonexclusive suggests that
    a. everyone will consume it.
    b. no one can be denied its use.
    c. it is easily privatized.
    d. it is of low quality.
    e. only the poor purchase it.

3. A nonrival good is one such that
    a. my consumption of the good doesn't deplete it for others to consume.
    b. it is the best of its kind on the market.
    c. the good has no close substitutes.
    d. its price elasticity will be very low.
    e. private firms will be likely to offer it in abundant quantities.

4. One of the problems associated with a public good is that
   a. private owners have no taste for these goods.
   b. the market will provide too much of them.
   c. chronic excess demand exists.
   d. people feel that because others want it, they personally won't have to pay for it.
   e. people enjoy them too much.

5. One can make a case that our international aid program is in part all the following except
   a. national security.
   b. Social Security.
   c. expression of our humanitarian concern.
   d. job creation.
   e. transfer payment.

6. The largest percentage of federal government spending is on
   a. purchases of goods and services.
   b. transfer payments.
   c. grants-in-aid to state and local governments.
   d. foreign aid.
   e. defense.

7. As a percentage of real GDP, spending on security in the United States from 1960 to 1990
   a. rose.
   b. fell.
   c. stayed the same.
   d. fluctuated wildly between presidential administrations.
   e. failed to keep up with inflation.

8. Government spending on education from 1960 to 1990 grew most rapidly for
   a. preschool children.
   b. elementary school children.
   c. inner-city schools.
   d. high school students.
   e. colleges and universities.

9. The largest share of spending on transportation is handled at the
   a. municipal level.
   b. state and local level.
   c. federal level.
   d. regional level.
   e. aerospace level.

10. Government spending on agriculture has been justified on the grounds that
    a. farm families deserve higher incomes than the market would provide.
    b. farm prices are rising so research and development needs to be financed.
    c. food prices can be kept low this way.
    d. no one would farm otherwise.
    e. farming is harder work than other occupations.

11. One difference between Medicaid and Aid to Families with Dependent Children is that
    a. Medicaid serves the elderly and AFDC serves the poor.
    b. Medicaid provides in-kind benefits while AFDC provides cash grants.
    c. AFDC gets people out of poverty while Medicaid hardly helps.
    d. AFDC is more wasteful.
    e. virtually everyone qualifies for Medicaid while AFDC is more restrictive.

12. Government insurance protects individuals from all of the following except
    a. income losses due to retirement.
    b. income losses due to unemployment.
    c. income losses due to disability.
    d. income losses due to unexpected deaths of breadwinners.
    e. income losses due to fires.

13. When Social Security transfers in the United States are compared to those in other developed countries as a percentage of GDP, the United States is spending
    a. somewhat less.
    b. about the same.
    c. an adequate amount.
    d. an inadequate amount.
    e. far more.

14. When government spending in the United States is compared to spending in other developed countries as a percentage of GDP, it is clear that
    a. spending levels in the United States are well above those in other countries.
    b. spending levels in the United States are near the bottom of the range that is observed.
    c. spending levels in the United States have risen much faster than in other countries.
    d. spending levels in the United States need to be cut.
    e. spending levels in the United States need to be increased.

15. The Peacock-Wiseman hypothesis predicts that the level of government spending tends to
    a. stabilize in periods of relative calm but rise sharply during national crises and remain at a higher level once the crisis is over.
    b. rise sharply during national crises, then drop off dramatically after the crises.
    c. grow at a steady rate as GDP increases.
    d. differ radically between economies that represent different cultural characteristics.
    e. be much higher than most individuals in industrialized countries would prefer.

Discussion Questions

1. What is meant by a public good? What is meant by a transfer payment?

2. Without looking at your text, list the items of government spending and indicate whether they are federal or state and local. As well, indicate whether they are significant or minor in terms of percent of total spending.

3. Explain why government spends on the farm community. Is this spending a public good, a transfer payment, or part of the government's countercyclical fiscal policy?

4. How does Social Security spending get financed in the United States? How is this system different from a private pension fund?

5. What is the Peacock-Wiseman hypothesis on government spending?

6. How does government spending influence the allocation of society's resources?

CHAPTER 14   GOVERNMENT SPENDING

Answers to Questions

True-False Questions

1. False because government spending is also a political decision.
2. True
3. True
4. True
5. False because they may not have saved sufficiently and anyway they receieve more than they have contributed.
6. False because interest payments are a growing percent of federal spending.
7. True
8. False because national defense spending as a perecent of total federal spending has fallen.
9. False because the space program is a public good.
10. True
11. False because food stamps can only be exchanged legally for food.
12. True
13. False because eligibility extends to the disabled and dependents of beneficiaries.
14. False because social insurance payments have increased by .7 percent per year while GDP has risen by 2.6 percent per year from 1960 to 1990.
15. True
16. False because the Peacock-Wiseman hypothesis suggests that government spending stays at a higher level than it had been prior to the crisis.
17. False because government spending is for goods and services that the market would not provide in sufficient quantities.

Multiple Choice Questions

1. d	6. b	11. b
2. b	7. b	12. e
3. a	8. e	13. a
4. d	9. b	14. b
5. b	10. a	15. a

Discussion Questions

1. Public goods are basically nonexclusive and nonrival. Nonexclusive means that no one can be excluded from consuming the good—like walking a city street or enjoying the security of national defense—and nonrival means that any person's consumption of that good does not diminish the good for other people—like walking that street doesn't lessens anybody else's use of that street. By contrast, umbrellas are not public goods because the owner can exclude others from using it, and when one uses it, it is not available to someone else at the same time. Transfer payments are payments by government to particular groups in society. These are in the form of price subsidies, payment of goods-in-find, or direct cash payments.

2. Check the text.

3. Government spending on the farm community is essentially a transfer payment. Government farm programs end up taxing nonfarming populations and giving the income to the farming population. Among the many reasons for the program—some political, of course—is the idea that since the 1930s, the farm economy has been in chronic depression because farm prices keep falling relative to nonfarming prices. The government's farm program was designed to save the farm community.

4. Social Security is financed by taxes paid jointly by employers and employees. People of working age pay for the benefits received by the current generation of retirees. Social Security differs from a private pension fund in three ways. First, Social Security is mandatory. Second, Social Security transfers income across income and age groups. A pension fund keeps funds that an individual deposits for that individual. Third, Social Security is a pay-as-you-go system financed by a payroll tax.

5. During a crisis, government spending rises to levels far above the typical range. People become used to the new level of government spending. What was once thought to be too high a level of government spending is perceived to be normal. As a result, after the crisis, government spending tends to stay at the new level.

6. When the government purchases goods and services, government purchases replace private sector purchases of goods and services. If the economy is at full employment, government purchases of goods and services come at the expense of private goods that might have been produced. In 1990, federal, state, and local purchases of goods and services amounted to just under 20 percent of GDP.

CHAPTER 15

FINANCING GOVERNMENT: TAXES AND DEBT

Chapter Summary

Public goods are not free goods. Resources are needed to produce city streets just as they are needed to produce automobiles that drive up and down those streets. The opportunity costs of producing public goods— measured by how much we must give up of private goods—is always a matter of public debate. But supposing that issue resolved— we know how much public goods we want and are willing to make the sacrifice to acquire them—the question still remains: How does the government get the money it needs to provide those public goods?

In pre-modern societies, it was often the case that a government would simply commandeer the resources it needed. If it needed labor to construct roads, it simply rounded up people to make the roads. The roads were built, but not necessarily in the most efficient way. In modern societies, government has shifted from commandeering resources to commandeering money. That's the essence of a tax system.

There are a number of ways to tax. Perhaps the simplest is a poll (or head) tax, say $100, that is levied on every adult in a population. If there are 1,000 people, then the government's tax revenue is $100,000. An alternative way of taxing the population is not by levying the tax on the person, but on the person's income. This is the income tax. An income tax structure can be regressive (the rich are taxed a lower percent of their income than are the poor), proportional (the rich and poor are taxed the same percent) or progressive (the rich are taxed a higher percent). The government can also levy taxes on corporate profits, or on wealth (such as a property tax or estate and gift taxes). Perhaps the most widely used tax is levied not on a person's income or wealth, but on the person's consumption (sales and excise taxes). Contributions to the Social Security system is another form of taxation, but these are earmarked to finance the benefits the Social Security system is obligated to pay.

What does the U.S. tax structure look like? At the federal level, the income tax is its most important source of revenue. Its structure is progressive, with five tax brackets. The richer you are, the higher the tax rate on your higher income.

Income bracket	Percent of income taxed	Of the amount over
$0 to $38,000	15	
$38,000 to $91,850	28	$38,000
$91,850 to $140,000	31	$91,850
$140,000 to $250,000	36	$140,000
$250,000 and over	39.6	$250,000

If you earn $100,000, you pay 15 percent on your first $38,000; 28 percent on the income over $38,000 up to $91,850; and 31 percent on the remaining $8,250.

Most states have their own state income tax, but these are not as important a contributor to state revenue as their sales tax. The property tax is the primary source of revenue for local governments. Between 1960 and 1991, federal, state, and local revenues nearly tripled in real terms. These increases, however, were still insufficient to cover total government spending.

How does government make up the difference? The chapter focuses on the federal government's use of debt financing. The government, through its Department of the Treasury, sells securities. These securities are its IOUs. People loan money to the government in return for an interest payment. (The rate of interest the government offers is competitive; otherwise they would have difficulty selling them.) The securities are regarded as very safe investments because the government has never defaulted on either interest or principal. The securities come in three forms: Treasury bills that mature within a year, Treasury notes that mature in two to ten years, and Treasury bonds that mature in 30 years.

The federal debt has risen enormously since 1929, particularly since the 1980s, but so has GDP. The debt/GDP ratio was lower in 1991, by about one-third, than at the end of World War II. Big spurts in the debt/GDP ratio occurred in the decades of the 1930s, the 1940s, and the 1980s. The debt/GDP ratio for the United States is similar to those in the OECD countries.

Government debt, like government deficits, is a contentious political issue. How much longer can the government finance its deficits by selling IOUs before it goes bankrupt? Are we placing a terrible financial burden on future generations?

Economists distinguish between an internally-financed debt (its securities are purchased by its own population) and an externally-financed debt (its securities are purchased by foreigners). An internal debt neither adds nor subtracts from the nation's income. If 100 percent of the U.S. government debt is held internally (by U.S. citizens), then all the interest that the government pays goes to Americans. Where does the government get the money to pay for the interest? By taxing its citizens. In a sense then, Americans tax themselves to pay themselves. What about future generations? If future generations are forced to pay for the debt, they pay it only to themselves. An external debt is different. The people who are taxed to pay the interest on the debt are not the same people who receive the interest payments. An external debt can burden future generations.

Internally-financed debt still causes problems. If the debt is held by few people, then everybody is taxed to pay the interest that goes to the few. In this way, it contributes to greater income inequality. It can also create over-consumption because people view their securities holdings as real wealth and save less than they perhaps should. It can also contribute to inflation and crowd out private investment.

Deficits and debt are not inevitable. A balanced budget requires that tax revenues match government spending. The extraordinary rise in the 1980s deficits and debt resulted from the tax reform acts of 1981 and 1986 that overhauled our tax rates and brackets, and with it, tax revenues. The Gramm-Rudman-Hollings Act of 1985 was intended to introduce discipline to the budgetary process by setting targets for deficit reduction. This act failed to achieve its goals. A Constitutional amendment that would mandate a year-by-year balanced budget continues to be discussed.

Key Terms — Test your comprehension by identifying and explaining the significance of these terms.

- commandeer
- poll tax
- regressive income tax
- proportional income tax
- progressive income tax
- corporate income tax
- property tax
- estate tax
- gift tax
- unit tax
- sales tax
- customs duty
- excise tax
- public debt
- crowding out
- external debt

CHAPTER 15 FINANCING GOVERNMENT: TAXES AND DEBT

True-False Questions — If a statement is false, explain why.

1. Because people don't pay directly for public goods, these goods are described by economists as free goods. (T/F)

2. Because a poll tax is levied on every adult in the population, it must be fair. (T/F)

3. The difference between a deficit and debt is that a deficit represents the accumulation of debts over many years while a debt represents the amount by which government spending exceeds tax revenues in a single year. (T/F)

4. When the rate of interest falls, the price of bonds increases, and vice-versa. (T/F)

5. Government bonds are issued by the Department of the Treasury and government notes and bills are issued by the Fed. (T/F)

6. By lowering deficits, government debt will decrease and with it the rate of interest. (T/F)

7. The largest holders of the U.S. public debt are foreigners, mainly Japanese and Saudi Arabians. (T/F)

8. The U.S. public debt in the early 1990s was over 100 percent of GDP. (T/F)

9. When your salary bonus moves you up a bracket in a progressive income tax structure, all your income is now taxed at the new, higher rate which is why most people complain. (T/F)

10. Compared to West European market countries, the tax/GDP ratio in the United States is relatively high. (T/F)

11. A principal difference between the income tax you pay and the contributions you make to Social Security is that your Social Security contributions are earmarked. (T/F)

12. The public debt consists of only one year's government securities which must be paid back at the end of the fiscal year. (T/F)

13. If our public debt is held internally, Americans make payments on the debt to themselves. (T/F)

14. By borrowing in order to finance its spending, the government can alter the mix of goods purchased by its population to include more public goods and less private goods. (T/F)

15. Federal Reserve purchases of government securities issued to finance a deficit can create inflation because it may contribute to the growth of the money supply. (T/F)

16. Crowding out refers to the decrease in private investment caused by the rise in the interest rate that accompanies debt finance by the government. (T/F)

17. As the evidence shows, the best way to decrease deficits and debt is through a series of supply-side tax cuts, like those implemented during President Reagan's administrations. (T/F)

18. The Gramm-Rudman-Hollings Act of 1985 called for across-the-board cuts in government spending if deficit reduction targets were not met. (T/F)

19. Today, we have a constitutional amendment that requires a balanced budget. (T/F)

20. The Clinton administration has played a more interventionist role in the economy by raising taxes and deciding which economic activities are taxed and which are not. (T/F)

Multiple Choice Questions

1. All of the following are examples of regressive taxes except
   a. the poll tax.
   b. excise taxes.
   c. sales taxes.
   d. customs duties.
   e. the proportional income tax.

2. The revenue from social security taxes is
   a. invested in a pension fund for each individual to draw on at retirement.
   b. earmarked for a trust fund out of which social security benefits are paid.
   c. never sufficient to pay all the benefits for retirees and other beneficiaries.
   d. handled in the same way that other tax revenues are handled.
   e. about equal to the revenue generated by gift and estate taxes.

3. Crowding out is the idea that as the government finances deficit spending by borrowing, it must
   a. lower interest rates, thus taking funds away from private investment.
   b. raise interest rates, thus taking funds away from private investment.
   c. shut private borrowers completely out of the market for investment funds.
   d. accept the lower growth rate in the economy that inevitably results.
   e. continually ask for higher and higher prices on the bonds it sells.

4. The national debt is a burden to future generations to the extent that a portion of the debt is held by
   a. foreigners.
   b. government institutions like the Social Security Trust Fund.
   c. nonfamily members.
   d. national banks.
   e. pension funds.

5. The primary source of revenue for general spending by the federal government is
   a. property taxes.
   b. income taxes.
   c. tariff revenues.
   d. inheritance taxes.
   e. corporate profits taxes.

6. The main problem with the accumulation of a public debt by running deficit budgets each year is that
   a. financing the deficit becomes more difficult each year because the nation's credit is deteriorating.
   b. interest rates have to be kept low so that the government can afford to borrow.
   c. the deficit is climbing to very high levels as a percentage of GDP.
   d. the government must pay a high interest rate to borrow and this tends to crowd out private investment.
   e. private investment is nearly always more efficient than public investment so most government activities should be turned over to the private sector.

7. Most of the federal debt, until the 1980s, has accumulated as a result of
   a. natural disasters.
   b. government spending that is grossly out of line with spending in other countries.
   c. wars and recessions.
   d. tax cuts.
   e. the absence of a balanced budget amendment to the Constitution.

8. The argument that the U.S. public debt is not a burden to future generations of Americans is correct insofar as the debt is held by
   a. the very rich.
   b. Americans with ownership of the debt spread evenly over the population.
   c. foreigners who are paid in dollars.
   d. international financial institutions like the World Bank.
   e. the Social Security trust fund.

9. One reason that the federal budget is so difficult to balance is that
   a. there are always unforeseen emergencies, such as earthquake relief, that demand unprogrammed government spending.
   b. people enjoy the benefits associated with government spending programs so that cuts are unpopular.
   c. there is very little wasteful spending that could be cut.
   d. even minor spending cuts and tax increases would be disastrous for the economy.
   e. the budget is far too complicated to expect balance to be achieved.

10. The largest owners of the U.S. public debt are
    a. federal agencies and trust funds.
    b. commercial banks.
    c. state and local governments.
    d. foreigners.
    e. individual U.S. citizens.

11. As a percentage of GDP, tax revenues in the United States
    a. are somewhat lower than in other industrialized countries.
    b. have ballooned since 1980.
    c. tend to decrease after a national emergency has been addressed.
    d. are about 50 percent.
    e. have stayed constant over our history.

12. A progressive income tax is one in which
    a. everyone pays the same rate.
    b. everyone must pay a fixed amount.
    c. the poor pay a larger percentage of their income than do the rich.
    d. the rich pay a larger percentage of their income than do the poor.
    e. consumption is discouraged.

13. The primary source of tax revenue for state governments is
    a. state income tax.
    b. estate and gift tax.
    c. sales tax.
    d. property tax.
    e. lottery revenue.

14. The burden of the U.S. public debt consists primarily of that portion of the debt that is owned by
    a. all U.S. citizens.
    b. U.S. commercial banks.
    c. foreigners.
    d. U.S. citizens who default on their share of the payments on the debt.
    e. U.S. future generations who inherit the debt.

15. Deficit finance can be inflationary if it is accomplished by
    a. purchases of government securities by foreigners.
    b. purchases of government securities by Americans.
    c. purchases of government securities by commercial banks.
    d. purchases of government securities by the Federal Reserve.
    e. tax increases.

16. When the government's countercyclical fiscal policy to combat recession creates a deficit that is financed internally, it can cause the following to happen except
    a. crowding out.
    b. greater income inequality.
    c. higher rates of unemployment.
    d. higher inflation.
    e. higher consumption spending.

17. Arranged from shortest to the longest maturity, the government securities are
    a. Treasury bills, Treasury notes, Treasury bonds.
    b. Treasury notes, Treasury bills, Treasury bonds.
    c. Treasury bonds, Treasury notes, Treasury bills.
    d. Treasury bonds, Treasury bills, Treasury notes.
    e. Treasury bills, Treasury bonds, Treasury notes.

18. The tax reforms of 1981 and 1986
    a. raised tax rates, but ended up reducing tax revenues.
    b. lowered tax rates that ended up reducing tax revenues.
    c. created additional tax brackets to capture revenue from the very rich.
    d. converted the income tax structure from progressive to proportional.
    e. eliminated federal sales tax, but increased the federal tax rates on inheritance.

19. While a property tax can be described as a proportional wealth tax, as a fraction of income the property tax is, in most cases,
    a. a flat tax.
    b. an income tax.
    c. a proportional tax.
    d. a progressive tax.
    e. a regressive tax.

20. One way that the United States' external debt could be reduced is for
    a. taxes to be increased.
    b. investment to increase.
    c. the government to buy up bonds that are held by foreigners.
    d. government spending to be cut.
    e. the government to sell bonds in foreign markets.

Discussion Questions

1. How does a progressive income tax differ from a proportional and regressive one? What argument can you make to show that the progressive tax is the fairest?

2. Suppose you were a debater and the topic was "Without recourse to public debt financing, the United States could not have financed the war against Germany and Japan". You took the affirmative. Make your case. Suppose you were given the negative, make the case.

3. Why is the U.S. public debt not a burden to the extent that it is held by other Americans? Does your answer depend on the distribution of the debt in the U.S.?

4. What was called for in the Gramm-Rudman-Hollings Act of 1985? Did it work? Why or why not?

5. Why do you suppose that commandeering resources was replaced by taxation as a method for government to acquire the means to provide public goods?

CHAPTER 15 FINANCING GOVERNMENT: TAXES AND DEBT

Answers to Questions

True-False Questions

1. False because there is an opportunity cost associated with the provision of public goods.
2. False because a poll tax is regressive.
3. False because the deficit is an increase in debt for one year while the debt is accumulated deficits over the years.
4. True
5. False because bills, notes and bonds are issued by the Department of the Treasury.
6. True
7. False because federal agencies and trust funds hold most of the debt.
8. False because it is approximately 60 percent.
9. False because only the amount earned over the bracket is taxed at the higher rate.
10. False because the U.S. tax/GDP ratio is relatively low.
11. True
12. False because the public debt is the accumulation of past deficits and these can be refinanced by issuing new debt.
13. True
14. True
15. True
16. True
17. False because the deficit increased dramatically during the Reagan years.
18. True
19. False because such an amendment is still under discussion.
20. True

Multiple Choice Questions

1. e	6. d	11. a	16. c
2. b	7. c	12. d	17. a
3. b	8. b	13. c	18. b
4. a	9. b	14. c	19. e
5. b	10. a	15. d	20. c

Discussion Questions

1. A progressive income tax is one in which the rich are taxed a higher percent of their income than are the poor. A proportional tax is one in which the rich and poor are taxed the same percent of income, and a regressive tax is one in which the poor are taxed a higher percent. The progressive tax may be considered fairest because it is supposed that the pain associated with the rich giving up, say, $100, is no more than the poor giving up, say, $10. If taxes are to represent equal burden across income classes, then the progressive structure is the fairest.

2. Affirmative: The means used to finance the war is not a real issue. Getting it financed in a quick and most responsive way is. If people believe that holding bonds gives them something in the future, fine! We need their money now to buy the military equipment to win the war. All we want to do is shift the economy's position along the production possibilities curve from civilian to military production. The sale of government securities accomplishes this with less opposition than, say, a tax.

    Negative: While the sale of securities does the job, it is more dishonest than financing the war through taxation. People ought to know what they are fighting for and what it means in terms of sacrificing civilian goods. A tax tells them that in no uncertain terms. The public debt is a deceiver because people think the securities they buy add to their total wealth, failing to realize that they eventually must pay themselves.

3. The debt is not a burden to the extent that one group of Americans is paying the interest and principal on the debt to another group of Americans. However, if the debt is held by the rich and the middle class and the poor pay taxes to finance the interest payments, then the debt can make the income distribution more unequal.

4. This act called for across-the-board cuts in federal government spending if certain specific deficit reduction targets were not met according to a timetable. However, it didn't work largely because cuts in government spending are so hard to achieve because many people benefit from the spending and fight the proposed cuts. The Gramm-Rudman-Hollings targets were typically relaxed and exceptions were made.

5. Commandeering resources is very complicated and you may not get the resources you need by commandeering them. As government became more complicated over human history, it is natural that money with its high liquidity would be the preferred form for payment of taxes to the government.

CHAPTER 16

INTERNATIONAL TRADE

Chapter Summary

If there is any consensus among economists, it's here: Free trade benefits everyone. Between any two countries, it's a win/win situation. Why? Ultimately, all trade is based on differences in costs of production. The opportunity costs of producing different goods—measured by the amount of other goods sacrificed—differs between regions within a country and between countries around the world. One reason for the differences in opportunity costs is the variation in natural resource endowments we find in different countries. You can't produce bananas at the North Pole. And you don't find polar bears in Costa Rica. Because of the geographic differences in these endowments, geographic specialization in producing particular goods occurs all over the world. By Canada's specializing in the production of a good that has a low opportunity cost of production and trading that good for goods that are more expensive to produce in Canada, Canadians improve their standard of living. What's true for Canada is true for Peru and every other country. While the gains from trade accrue for every country as a whole, some people in each country stand to lose. Why? If the U.S. trades with Brazil, Americans may enjoy lower coffee prices, but coffee producers in the U.S. will probably have to find other jobs. Resources in the U.S. (and Brazil) will shift to production of those goods whose opportunity costs are relatively low.

The advantages that give rise to specialization come in two forms. *Absolute advantage* describes a situation in which one country is absolutely more efficient than another in producing a good (it requires fewer resources to produce it). Specialization and trade make sense under these circumstances. Another type of advantage is *comparative advantage*. In this situation, a country is relatively more efficient than another country in producing the good. Relative efficiency is measured by the opportunity cost of producing the good. For example, Canada may use more resources to produce a bushel of wheat than does the U.S., but the opportunity cost of producing the bushel in the U.S. might be higher—what is has to give up in order to produce that bushel. It may pay, then, for the U.S. to let Canadians produce the wheat even though more resources are actually used in its production.

The gains from trade—stemming from either absolute or comparative advantage—are shared by both of the trading countries if, for each country, the prices of the two goods traded fall between the pre-trade opportunity costs of producing them at home. Economists measure how much each of the trading countries gains from trade by calculating their *terms of trade*. A country's terms of trade is the ratio of its export prices to its import prices.

In this respect, although less-developed countries (LDCs) gain from trade, they suffer a disadvantage compared to industrially advanced countries. Their disadvantage owes to the fact that most of their production is focused on agricultural goods and raw materials that have low and falling prices. These goods are the LDCs' export goods. However, the goods they import tend to have high and rising prices. The terms of trade, then, work against them. In recent years, they have experienced moderate to significant deterioration in their terms of trade. On the other hand, the terms of trade for industrialized countries improved in the vast majority of cases over recent years.

The world's economies are becoming increasingly interrelated. More than 15 percent of the world's 1993 GDP made its way onto international markets in the form of exports and imports. That compares to less than three percent in 1970. For the most part, the industrialized countries trade with each other and developing countries increasingly trade with the industrialized countries. The developed economies in 1993 absorbed some 70 percent of their own exports and over 57 percent of the exports of LDCs. The primary trade partners for the United States are, in order, Canada, Japan, and Mexico. Together, Canada and Mexico dwarf trade between the United States and other countries. The enormous trade flow on the North American continent stands to reason because of the proximity of the United States to Canada and Mexico.

Many arguments are made against free trade but these are always made as exceptions to the rule. Arguments against free trade address particular circumstances. For example, these arguments include the need to produce our own military goods so that we do not depend on others for our national survival, the need to protect our infant industries, the need to protect our workers from cheap foreign labor, the need to diversify our industries, the need to protect our industries against dumping (selling below cost) by other countries, and the need to retaliate against other countries' restrictions on trade.

Tariffs and *quotas* are instruments of trade control. A tariff is simply a tax on an imported good. A tariff causes the foreign price of the good in a domestic market to rise above the domestic price so that domestic manufacturers with higher costs of production can gain a larger share of the domestic market. Quotas accomplish the same without creating a revenue for the government as a tariff does. With a quota, foreign manufacturers reap a windfall from the increase in price that the quota creates. Nontariff barriers are also used to restrict imports. There may be quality restrictions imposed on particular goods that are designed to block most imports.

Tariff structures are typically negotiated between countries. The notion of reciprocity plays an important role in the nature of tariff structures. Reciprocity means that any tariff structure negotiated between two countries also applies to their other trading partners. In this way, tariff structures are nondiscriminating. Under the General Agreement on Tariffs and Trade (GATT), the nondiscriminating character of the tariff structure is accomplished through the most-favored nation clause. Any reduction in a tariff offered to one country must be offered to all. Tariff barriers to trade have gradually been reduced under GATT and the latest round of negotiations led to reductions in nontariff barriers to trade. GATT offers concessions to less-developed countries by allowing them to impose tariffs on imports from industrialized countries while giving LDCs most-favored nation status on their exports. Other tariff structures are customs unions and free trade areas. A customs union such as the European Economic Community permits free trade within the union and a common tariff schedule with countries not in the union. A free trade area permits free trade within the area and allows members to develop their own tariff policies with nonmembers. The North American Free Trade Agreement (NAFTA) is an example of a free trade area.

United States tariff rates have fluctuated significantly over time. Especially high tariff rates were operative from 1870 to 1890 and during the 1920s. However, since 1934 the tariff rate in the United States has fallen steadily so that the average tariff rate in the United States in 1987 was just six percent. Compared to other industrialized countries, the United States is not very protectionist.

Key Terms — Test your comprehension by defining and explaining the significance of these terms.

free trade	tariff
international specialization	quota
absolute advantage	reciprocity
comparative advantage	General Agreement on Tariffs and Trade (GATT)
imports	customs union
exports	European Economic Community (EEC)
terms of trade	free trade area
dumping	North American Free Trade Agreement (NAFTA)

True-False Questions — If a statement is false, explain why.

1. If the opportunity costs of producing two goods differ between two countries, then specialization and free trade will benefit both countries. (T/F)

2. If the endowment of natural resources was the same in every country, there would be fewer opportunities for specialization and trade. (T/F)

3. To say that both countries engaged in free trade benefit is to say that everyone in both countries benefits. (T/F)

4. If Canada has an absolute advantage over Ireland in producing fish and fowl, it means that Canada used fewer resources to produce both than Ireland. (T/F)

5. If the opportunity cost of producing a good is higher in the United States than in Japan, then the United States has a comparative advantage in that area. (T/F)

6. If two countries specialize and trade, then the price of goods traded should fall between the before-trade prices in both countries in order for both to share in the gains from trade. (T/F)

7. The terms of trade equation for Mexico is the index of Mexican export prices divided by the index for Mexican import prices multiplied by 100. (T/F)

8. The world's industrialized countries buy most of their imports from less developed countries because labor costs there are so much lower. (T/F)

9. The terms of trade have improved radically for most developing countries in recent years. (T/F)

10. The volume of imports and exports is larger for Japan than for any other country. (T/F)

11. The United States' largest trading partner is Canada. (T/F)

12. The national security argument against free trade holds that goods vital to a nation's security should be produced domestically. (T/F)

13. The infant industry argument holds that protection should be withdrawn once an industry has had sufficient time to acquire expertise and experience. (T/F)

14. Dumping involves selling exports below cost in order to drive foreign competitors out of the market. (T/F)

15. Tariffs provide domestic producers with a greater share of the domestic market, but domestic consumers end up paying a higher price for the tariff-protected goods. (T/F)

16. As a mechanism to raise revenue for the government, quotas are more effective than tariffs. (T/F)

17. Reciprocity involves granting any tariff reductions offered to one country to all other trading partners. (T/F)

18. If a country is a most-favored nation under the GATT, then tariff rates for that country are zero. (T/F)

19. The European Economic Community is an example of a customs union whereas the North American Free Trade Agreement is an example of a free trade area. (T/F)

20. Tariff rates in the United States have been consistently low since 1860. (T/F)

Multiple Choice Questions

1. If it takes Mexico 40 labor hours to produce a barrel of wine and 30 labor hours to produce a bushel of corn, then
   a. Mexico could not benefit from international trade.
   b. Mexico has an absolute advantage in wine production.
   c. Mexico has a comparative advantage in wine production.
   d. the opportunity cost of 1 barrel of wine is 4/3 bushel of corn.
   e. the opportunity cost of 1 bushel of corn is 4/3 barrel of wine.

2. The best way for a country to restrict trade in the international market for lawnmowers is to
   a. impose a tariff on imported lawnmowers.
   b. set a price floor on imported lawnmowers.
   c. set a price ceiling.
   d. impose a tariff on exports of lawnmowers.
   e. set a quota on the quantity of lawnmowers that can be exported.

3. A country's terms of trade is the ratio
   a. of the quantity of its exports to the quantity of its imports.
   b. of the value of its exports to the value of its imports.
   c. of the index of its export prices to the index of its import prices, multiplied by 100.
   d. of domestic prices to international prices, multiplied by 100.
   e. of prices protected by tariffs to those prices subject to free trade.

4. An arrangement which permits free trade among member countries, but in which each is allowed to establish its own tariff policy with respect to nonmembers, is known as
   a. reciprocity.
   b. a free trade area.
   c. trading blocs.
   d. a fixed exchange rate.
   e. a customs union.

5. The infant industries argument
   a. promotes indiscriminate free trade.
   b. claims to protect a new industry with unskilled labor.
   c. is used by most countries to protect textiles, especially children's wear.
   d. calls for lower tariff rates on imports.
   e. supports the protection of newly established industries from foreign competition.

CHAPTER 16   INTERNATIONAL TRADE

Questions 6 and 7 relate to the following table.

	United States	Switzerland
	Labor time to produce:	
1 pair of skis	10 hours	8 hours
1 pound of chocolate	2 hours	1 hour

6. The data in the table show that
   a. Switzerland has the absolute advantage in producing both goods.
   b. the United States has the absolute advantage in producing both goods.
   c. the Swiss have a comparative advantage in chocolate production.
   d. the United States has a comparative advantage in ski production.
   e. there is no clear trade advantage for either country.

7. The opportunity costs of producing one pound of chocolate in each country are
   a. United States—1/5 pair of skis; Switzerland—1/8 pair of skis.
   b. United States—5 pairs of skis; Switzerland—8 pairs of skis.
   c. United States—4/5 pair of skis; Switzerland—1/2 pair of skis.
   d. United States—5/4 pairs of skis; Switzerland—2 pairs of skis.
   e. United States—1/4 pair of skis; Switzerland—1/10 pair of skis.

8. All of the following are classic arguments against indiscriminate free trade except
   a. the national security argument.
   b. the mature industries argument.
   c. the cheap foreign labor argument.
   d. the diversity of industry argument.
   e. the antidumping argument.

9. The argument for trade protection which involves maintaining many different industries is known as
   a. cheap labor.
   b. infant industries.
   c. republican.
   d. retaliation.
   e. the diversity of industry argument.

10. A country's ability to produce a good at a lower opportunity cost than the country it trades with is its
    a. superiority.
    b. absolute advantage.
    c. international specialization.
    d. comparative advantage.
    e. dumping.

11. All of the following are arguments for trade restrictions except
    a. retaliation.
    b. country specialization.
    c. cheap labor.
    d. strategic trade.
    e. national security.

Questions 12 and 13 relate to the following table.

Hours of Labor to Produce an Automobile or a Computer

	U.S.	France
Auto	120	90
Computer	50	10

12. France's opportunity cost of producing one computer is
    a. 1/9 auto.
    b. 9 autos.
    c. 1/5 auto.
    d. 9/12 auto.
    e. 1/12 auto.

13. If trade takes place between the U.S. and France, the price of autos, in terms of computers, must fall between
    a. 5/8 and 3/4.
    b. 4/3 and 1/2.
    c. 3/4 and 2/1.
    d. 5/12 and 1/9.
    e. 12/5 and 9.

14. If the opportunity cost of producing onions is lower in Montana than in Ohio, then Montana has
    a. a comparative advantage over Ohio.
    b. an absolute advantage over Ohio.
    c. no significant advantage.
    d. highly skilled onion farmers.
    e. a much better climate for farming than Ohio.

15. Free trade between Canada and the United States
    a. helps every Canadian and American.
    b. generally hurts one country and helps the other.
    c. allows for production specialization in Canada and the United States.
    d. is more beneficial to the larger country, United States.
    e. is more beneficial to the smaller country, Canada.

16. North American Free Trade Agreement (NAFTA)
    a. protects the United States from cheap labor production in Mexico.
    b. created free trade between Canada and the U.S., but protected both from Mexican cheap labor production.
    c. created a free trade area which includes Canada, United States, and Mexico.
    d. created a customs union, similar to the European Community, in Canada and the United States.
    e. created a customs union, similar to the European Community, in Canada, United States, and Mexico.

17. Most international trade takes place
    a. among the industrially developed countries, who trade with each other.
    b. between the industrially developed countries, who export, and the less-developed countries (LDCs), who import.
    c. between the LDCs who export raw materials and the industrially developed who import raw materials.
    d. among the LDCs because they are mostly young, dynamic economies, such as Korea and Hong Kong.
    e. among the LDCs because they have the largest populations, such as India, China, and Brazil.

18. The United States government will place a quota on wheat
    a. to restrict the quantity of wheat U.S. wheat producers can sell abroad.
    b. to raise government revenues from imports of wheat to the United States.
    c. to restrict the quantity of wheat that can be imported.
    d. to shift the domestic supply curve to the right in order to lower domestic wheat prices.
    e. to shift the domestic supply curve to the left in order to raise domestic wheat prices.

19. In the case of free trade between two countries, the supply curve facing consumers in the importing country will be
    a. comprised entirely by imported goods.
    b. perfectly elastic at the world price.
    c. pushed far to the right with the introduction of imports.
    d. quite stable over time.
    e. positively sloped.

20. The main difference between a free trade area and a customs union is that
    a. the former includes all countries in the western hemisphere and the latter only includes France, Germany, Italy, Holland, Belgium and Luxembourg.
    b. the former requires tariffs for all members and the latter does not.
    c. the former does not require tariffs for all members while the latter does.
    d. the former allows free trade among members and individual tariff policies to be applied to nonmembers, while the latter allows free trade for members and a common tariff for nonmembers.
    e. the former uses quotas for members and tariffs for nonmembers, and the latter uses tariffs for members and quotas for nonmembers.

Problems

1. Suppose that in one hour the United States can produce 180 computer microprocessors or 220 bushels of rice and that in Japan in one hour it is possible to produce 160 microprocessors or 120 bushels of rice.

   a. What is the opportunity cost of a microprocessor in the United States? In Japan? Who should specialize in microprocessor production? In rice production? Show your work.

   b. Suppose that these two countries begin to trade and that the price of one computer microprocessor is equal to one bushel of rice after trade. Draw a graph to show each country's production possibilities prior to trade and the line that represents the one-to-one ratio at which microprocessors and rice exchange for each other after trade. Carefully explain how the consumption opportunities have changed for each country as a result of trade.

   c. Identify which groups win and which groups lose as a result of trade in each country.

2. The following questions refer to the diagrams.

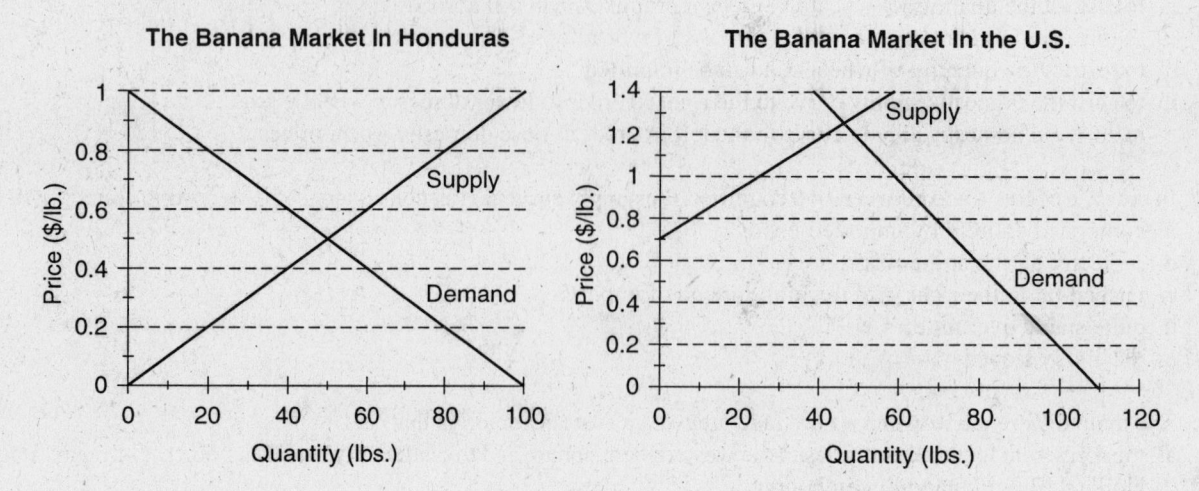

The Banana Market In Honduras

The Banana Market In the U.S.

a. Is there the potential for trade in bananas between Honduras and the United States? Which country will import and which will export? Explain why.

b. If there is the potential for trade, what will be the volume of exports and imports? What will be the after-trade price of bananas in both countries?

c. Suppose that the United States imposes a $0.20/lb. tariff on imported bananas. How will this effect the volume of bananas imported, if at all? Will this tariff generate any revenue? If so how much? Would it be possible to accomplish the same goals with a quota? Why or why not?

Discussion Questions

1. List and critique the arguments opposed to free trade.

2. Why are developing countries at a disadvantage in the terms of their trade with industrialized countries?

3. What's the difference between a customs union and a free trade area? If you were given a choice, which type of arrangement would you prefer to operate under? Why?

4. How would you explain the fact that most of the industrialized world's trade is within the industrialized countries?

Answers to Questions

True-False Questions

1. True
2. True
3. False because those in nonspecialty lines of production will be hurt by international trade at least in the short run.
4. True
5. False because Japan will have the comparative advantage in this case.
6. True
7. True
8. False because the industrialized countries trade mostly with each other.
9. False because the terms of trade have deteriorated for many developing countries in recent years.
10. False because the volume of trade is higher for the United States.
11. True
12. True
13. True
14. True
15. True
16. False because tariffs, not quotas, raise revenues for the government.
17. True
18. False because most-favored nation status means that any tariff reduction granted to one GATT member must be offered to them all.
19. True
20. False because tariff rates have fluctuated greatly since 1860.

Multiple Choice Questions

1. d	6. a	11. b	16. c
2. a	7. a	12. a	17. a
3. c	8. b	13. e	18. c
4. b	9. e	14. a	19. b
5. e	10. d	15. c	20. d

Problems

1. a. The opportunity cost of a microprocessor in the United States is 11/9 bushels of rice. The opportunity cost of a microprocessor in Japan is 3/4 bushel of rice. The United States should specialize in rice production and Japan should specialize in microprocessor production.

   b. Before trade in one hour the United States production possibilities frontier has endpoints showing that it is possible to produce either 180 microprocessors or 220 bushels of rice. After trade the microprocessor intercept shifts so that the United States can exchange rice for up to 220 microprocessors. Similarly, before trade Japan can produce either 160 microprocessors or 120 bushels of rice. After trade, Japan is able to exchange microprocessors for up to 160 bushels of rice. (See the following graphs.)

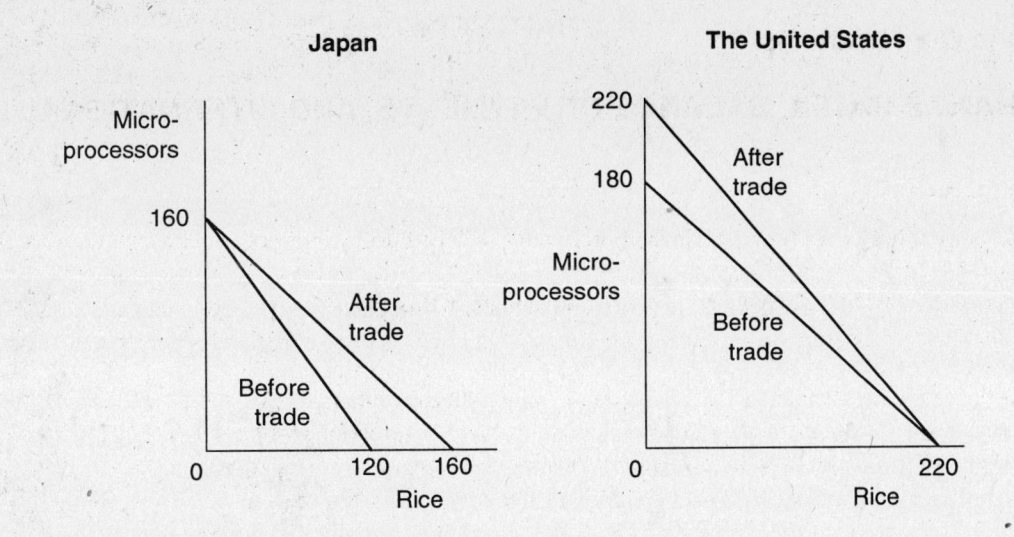

c. In the United States, rice farmers gain an immediate advantage as a result of trade while microprocessor producers are hurt. In Japan, rice farmers lose and microprocessor producers gain.

2. a. Honduras will export bananas to the United States since the equilibrium price is higher in the United States.

b. Honduras will export 60 lbs. of bananas to the United States. The price in Honduras will rise from $.50/lb. to $.80/lb. The price in the United States will fall from $1.20/lb. to $.80/lb.

c. A $.20/lb. tariff raises the U.S. price to $1.00/lb. Domestic producers will supply 30 lbs. of bananas and Honduras will export 30 lbs. Revenue from the tariff is 30 lbs. times $.20/lb. or $6.00.

Discussion Questions

1. These arguments are clearly explained in the text. Remember that each one is presented as an exception to the rule that free trade is preferred. Therefore, each argument must be justified on grounds that constitute special circumstances.

2. Developing countries are at a disadvantage because their export goods are typically agricultural goods and other natural resources the prices of which tend to be quite volatile. Over the years, the supply curve for agricultural goods has increased (shifted dramatically to the right) while the demand curve has increased only slightly. The result is a fall in the price of agricultural goods relative to industrial goods. In the industrially advanced countries, the opposite has happened. Demand curve for their goods increased dramatically. Prices have risen relative to agricultural goods.

3. A customs union requires that any tariff reduction granted to one member must be granted to all members and a common tariff policy with respect to nonmembers. A free trade area requires free trade among members and allows each member to establish its own tariff structure with respect to nonmembers. Given a choice, most would probably prefer the free trade area system since it grants participants more freedom to structure a tariff policy.

4. Industrialized countries trade with each other for the most part for reasons of taste and technology. Consider Americans' demands for goods and services. We are much more likely to have strong preferences for consumer electronics products from other industrialized countries than for the handicraft items produced in the developing world. Technology drives our tastes to some degree. We have tastes for sophisticated consumer electronics because we are a technologically advanced society.

CHAPTER 17

EXCHANGE RATES, BALANCE OF PAYMENTS, AND INTERNATIONAL DEBT

Chapter Summary

Every country has its own currency. When people from one country want to buy goods from another country, they discover that the seller of the good wants to be paid in his or her own currency. But how does the buyer acquire that currency? He must buy it before he buys the good. But at what price? Is there a market for currencies? That's what this chapter's about.

Because people engage in international trade, there are foreign exchange markets where currencies are traded for each other. The price of a currency measured in some other currency is called the *exchange rate*. Exchange rates are prices that, like all other prices, depend on demand and supply. The demand curve for a currency, say a French franc, priced in some other currency, say the U.S. dollar, is a downward-sloping curve. After all, the fewer dollars required to purchase a franc, the larger the quantity of French wine demanded by Americans and therefore the larger the quantity of French francs demanded. Conversely, the supply curve for francs priced in dollars is upward sloping. The more dollars the French receive for a franc, the larger the quantity of American goods they demand, which means the larger is their supply of francs to buy U.S. dollars.

The demand for a currency is influenced by several factors. For example, an increase in U.S. income raises the demand curve for French francs. Why? Because we have more income, we buy more goods, including French goods. Tastes also matter. If you enjoy French wine, you must demand French francs. Interest rates matter as well. If interest rates in France rise relative to those in the U.S., we want to buy French IOUs which means we need francs.

An increase in the supply of francs causes the dollar price of francs to fall. When world currencies are bought and sold in the foreign exchange markets, the array of exchange rates that emerge is said to be floating, meaning that they are free to adjust to changes in the demand and supply conditions for international markets, and the currencies to buy them.

Our currency, the U.S. dollar, appreciates relative to others if it takes fewer dollars to buy the others. It depreciates when it takes more of them to buy other currencies. Dollar appreciation is more commonly referred to as "strengthening the dollar." When it depreciates, it is considered "weakening."

Floating exchange rates create some degree of uncertainty to international trade. Why? Because you may decide to buy French wine when the exchange rate is 4 francs to the dollar and discover when the trade is actually made that the exchange rate changed to 2 francs to the dollar. The price of wine, for you, has just doubled! Risks stemming from exchange rate uncertainty create caution and reduce the volume of trade that would otherwise occur if there was no uncertainty about the exchange rate.

Fixed exchange rates represent an attempt to deal with the uncertainty associated with floating exchange rates. Governments simply freeze or fix exchange rates. So long as the fixed exchange rate is the same as the equilibrium or floating rate, there is no problem. But if the demand for francs increases, the price of the franc should rise. If it's fixed at the lower rate, government must satisfy the excess demand for the franc by providing francs on the market at that lower rate. Where does it get the francs? Governments hold stocks of *foreign exchange reserves*. This works only as long as the government's foreign exchange reserves don't run out. If it does, the government will have to (re)fix the rate at a lower price. That is called devaluation of the currency. Import controls are another means of maintaining the fixed rate. Here government limits the volume of imports to lessen the demand for foreign currencies. Imposing exchange controls forces domestic exporters to turn over supplies of foreign currencies at the fixed exchange rate in order to replenish the government's supplies of the foreign currencies. As a last resort, governments may borrow foreign currencies in order to maintain their foreign exchange reserves. Borrowing leads to international debt.

An economy's *balance of payments* account is a statement of its financial transactions with the rest of the world. The balance of payments account consists of both a *current account* and a *capital account.* The current account reflects the country's balance of trade—the difference between merchandise exports and merchandise imports—and differences between exports and imports of services, income receipts and payments, and unilateral transfers. The capital account consists of changes in assets held abroad by Americans and changes in foreign-held assets in the United States.

The United States balance of trade has been negative since 1975. A negative current account balance is offset (aside from statistical discrepancies) by a positive capital account balance. The dollars that flow out of the United States on the negative current account balance are matched by dollars that flow back to the United States on the positive capital account balance. It is no accident. The U.S. has to pay for its import surplus somehow, and if it borrows to pay for it, that borrowing shows up as an inflow of dollars into the U.S. capital accounts.

A balance of payments problem arises when, to a degree that is undesirable, we finance our negative current account balance by one or a combination of three methods. These are drawing down our foreign currency reserves, selling our assets for foreign currencies, and borrowing foreign currencies. Trade imbalances don't necessarily lead to problems. For example, it may be appropriate for a developing country to run a negative current account balance in order to acquire capital equipment from abroad to diversify its exports in the future. Deficits on the current account can also arise as a consequence of the strength of an economy. Foreigners investing in the United States because of its attractiveness will increase the value of the dollar, making foreign goods attractive to American consumers. Similarly, high interest rates in the United States may cause the dollar to appreciate and increase the current account deficit. A government budget deficit has the same effect. However, it may be that the current account deficit is a reflection of low productivity in the United States relative to other countries. If American industries cannot compete in foreign markets, then it stands to reason that a current account deficit will arise.

When countries borrow to acquire foreign exchange reserves, they incur international debt. International debt can burden an economy, especially a developing economy, when the debt service—the ratio of interest payments on the debt to the economy's exports—rises to high levels. In the long run, a current account deficit will lead to a depreciation in that country's currency so that imports become less attractive and the country's exports become more attractive. The currency depreciation will eventually bring the current account into balance. However, for a developing economy, the depreciation of its currency may be particularly painful if it is accompanied by a decline in living standards.

Key Terms — Test your comprehension by defining and explaining the significance of these terms.

foreign exchange market
exchange rate
floating exchange rate
appreciation
depreciation
arbitrage
fixed exchange rate
foreign exchange reserves
import controls
exchange controls

balance of payments
balance on current account
balance of trade
unilateral transfers
balance on capital account
international debt
debt service
external debt
devaluation

True-False Questions — If a statement is false, explain why.

1. The foreign exchange market deals with the international trade of goods and services. (T/F)

2. An exchange rate is a price at which one currency exchanges for another. (T/F)

3. As a nation's income increases, its demand for imports increases creating an increase in its demand for foreign currencies. (T/F)

4. A currency appreciates if it requires more of that currency to buy another. (T/F)

5. The supply curve for a currency will shift to the right when interest rates in that country fall relative to interest rates in other countries. (T/F)

6. Generally, it is bad for a country to have a weak currency. (T/F)

7. Arbitrage is the process whereby the exchange of currencies for one another tends to bring the exchange rates of many currencies into line with each other. (T/F)

8. One problem with a fixed exchange rate is that, if the demand for imports increases, an excess demand for the foreign currency will be generated at the fixed exchange rate. (T/F)

9. An exchange control system requires exporters to convert any foreign exchange earned by trade into the domestic currency in order to replenish the government's supply of foreign exchange. (T/F)

10. The balance of payments account shows whether or not a country is running a government budget deficit. (T/F)

11. Exports of goods and services and income receipts on investments from the rest of the world represent dollar inflows in the balance on current account. (T/F)

12. The value of exports minus the value of imports is the balance of trade. (T/F)

13. For an American to take a vacation in Cancun has the same effect on Mexico's current accounts as a Mexican exporting goods and services to the United States. (T/F)

14. The capital account shows changes in the capital stock of all industries within a country. (T/F)

15. Foreign investment in the United States represents a capital inflow to the United States. (T/F)

CHAPTER 17   EXCHANGE RATES

16. Trade imbalances always create economic problems at home. (T/F)

17. A strong dollar is likely to lead to a negative balance on the current account. (T/F)

18. To the extent that a country's budget deficit requires a high interest rate to finance it, it will tend to strengthen the country's currency. (T/F)

19. Low productivity contributes to a trade surplus by making the domestic producers' goods relatively cheaper than goods from other countries. (T/F)

20. LDCs incur international debt when they borrow in order to finance deficits on the current account. (T/F)

21. A country can only run a deficit on the current account for so long before the strength of its currency starts to diminish and imports become relatively more expensive while exports become relatively cheaper for other countries. (T/F)

Multiple Choice Questions

1. One effect of an appreciation of the U.S. dollar is that
   a. it contributes to employment in the U.S.
   b. we can buy imports more cheaply.
   c. our real income decreases.
   d. foreigners will demand more of our exports.
   e. our labor will become less productive.

2. The supply curve of U.S. dollars on the foreign exchange market reflects
   a. the willingness of the U.S. to supply goods and services on the international market.
   b. the willingness of foreigners to demand U.S. goods and services on the international market.
   c. the willingness of the U.S. to demand foreign goods and services on the international market.
   d. the willingness of foreigners to demand U.S. dollars on the foreign exchange market.
   e. the net exports (exports minus imports) that U.S. producers sell on the international market.

3. All of the following are useful options for the government to pursue to bolster foreign exchange reserves except
   a. impose exchange controls.
   b. impose export controls.
   c. adjust the exchange rate.
   d. borrow foreign currencies.
   e. impose a free floating exchange rate.

4. An example of dollar inflows on the balance of payments current account is
   a. the export of services.
   b. the income tax.
   c. changes in U.S. assets abroad.
   d. the income payments on foreign investments.
   e. the import of services

5. The difference between the value of a nation's merchandise exports and its merchandise imports is its
    a. external debt.
    b. balance on capital account.
    c. balance of trade.
    d. foreign exchange reserves.
    e. foreign exchange rate.

6. The U.S. exchange rate measures
    a. the ratio of the U.S.'s total exports to its total imports.
    b. the ratio of the U.S.'s value of total exports to its value of total imports.
    c. how many units of another country's currency can be bought with a U.S. dollar.
    d. the change in the value of a dollar vis-a-vis the change in the value of another currency.
    e. the difference between the value of the U.S. dollar and the value of another currency.

7. The U.S. balance of trade is computed by
    a. subtracting the value of U.S. imports from the value of U.S. exports.
    b. adding the U.S. current account to its capital account.
    c. balancing favorable and unfavorable exports and imports.
    d. adding all items that were exchanged (pluses and minuses) with other countries during a calendar year.
    e. subtracting foreign exchange rates from its own.

8. An unfavorable balance of trade can be financed in all the following ways except by
    a. drawing down reserves of foreign currencies.
    b. selling domestic assets to foreigners.
    c. selling government securities to foreigners.
    d. buying government securities from foreigners.
    e. borrowing the foreign currency.

9. Arbitrage is defined as
    a. the purchase of foreign currency.
    b. the purchase of foreign currency to give as gifts to relatives.
    c. buying a foreign currency in a market at a low price and selling it in another market at a higher price.
    d. the purchase of large quantities of one's own currency to sell in foreign markets.
    e. the act of buying a foreign currency in a market at a low price and selling it in another market at an even lower price.

10. One consequence of an appreciation in a country's exchange rate is
    a. its exports decrease.
    b. its imports decrease.
    c. its demand for foreign currencies increases.
    d. other countries, in response, must appreciate theirs.
    e. its government's foreign exchange reserves increase.

11. One consequence of a depreciation in a country's exchange rate is
    a. its demand for foreign currencies increases.
    b. its exports decrease.
    c. its imports decrease.
    d. other countries, in response, must appreciate theirs.
    e. its government's foreign exchange reserves increase.

12. The demand for U.S. dollars on the foreign exchange market will increase when
    a. U.S. incomes increase.
    b. foreign incomes decrease.
    c. interest rates in the rest of the world rise dramatically while U.S. rates remain unchanged.
    d. U.S. interest rates rise dramatically while those in the rest of the world remain unchanged.
    e. U.S. exports increase.

13. In an economy's balance of payments account
    a. the capital and current accounts must add to one.
    b. the current account is always greater than the capital account.
    c. both the current account and balance account are zero.
    d. the capital plus current account balances must equal zero.
    e. capital outflows must equal capital inflows.

14. Floating exchange rates refer to
    a. the ability of exchange rates to even out when displaced by shocks to the foreign exchange market.
    b. new issues of foreign exchange offered on the market.
    c. an exchange rate determined by the demand for and supply of a nation's currency.
    d. an excess demand for a nation's currency that creates its devaluation.
    e. an excess supply of a nation's currency that creates its appreciation.

15. Fixed exchange rates were designed to
    a. increase a nation's exports, if the fixed rate is low enough.
    b. reduce a nation's imports, if the fixed rate is high enough.
    c. reduce uncertainties to international trade associated with floating exchange rates.
    d. strengthen the nation's currency by curtailing the import of other currencies.
    e. provide government with revenues.

16. If Elrod studies in a foreign country and his parents send him $75, the money is a(n)
    a. private unilateral transfer.
    b. government income transfer.
    c. income payment on investment.
    d. capital account payment.
    e. service export.

17. All the following are part of the current account except
    a. merchandise exports.
    b. service exports.
    c. unilateral transfers.
    d. changes in foreign assets in the United States.
    e. income payments on investments.

18. Debt service measures
    a. interest payments on international debt as a percent of a nation's merchandise exports.
    b. the outflows from a nation's capital account to pay for imports of foreign services.
    c. the outflows from a nation's current account to pay for imports of foreign services.
    d. debt owed to a nation for the export of its services.
    e. international debt representing all the services transacted on all nations' balance of payments accounts.

19. A potential problem with free floating exchange rates is that
    a. currency speculators will gain from the losses of others.
    b. uncertainty in exchange rate fluctuations will cause international trade to be too risky.
    c. exchange rates will never tend toward an equilibrium.
    d. the currency markets will be monopolized.
    e. developing countries will always issue too much currency.

20. Some countries may not worry about a deficit on current account because
    a. they know they can always borrow to cover the deficit.
    b. they import capital goods to build up export industries that will eventually wipe out the deficits.
    c. deficits are always a stimulant to economic growth which is a higher priority.
    d. they can, if necessary, fix the exchange rate to wipe out the deficit.
    e. their capital account will be favorable since the balance of payments always ends up at zero.

Problems

1. Suppose that the exchange rate between the yen and the dollar is 80 yen per dollar and the rate between German marks and the dollar is 3 marks per dollar, while the rate between the yen and the mark is 20 yen per mark.

   a. Are these exchange rates mutually consistent? Why or why not?

   b. Is it possible to take 1000 yen and exchange them for marks and make further trades of currencies in this market at a profit? If so, how much profit can be made? Show your work.

   c. Will these exchange rates remain at their current levels? Explain.

Discussion Questions

1. a. Why is the demand curve for dollars priced in Mexican pesos downward sloping?

   b. Why is the supply curve of dollars priced in pesos upward sloping?

CHAPTER 17 EXCHANGE RATES   THE WORLD ECONOMY   167

2. Draw a supply and demand diagram for the market for dollars priced in pesos. Label the equilibrium price at 5 pesos per dollar. Suppose the demand for dollars increases so that the equilibrium price for dollars is 7 pesos per dollar. Has the peso appreciated or depreciated? Which currency has strengthened? Is this good or bad?

3. Suppose that in order to halt the dollar's decline relative to the yen, the United States Treasury introduces a new fixed exchange rate of 100 yen per dollar. However, the equilibrium exchange rate is 80 yen per dollar.

   a. Sketch a graph to show the supply and demand of dollars priced in yen under these circumstances. Is there an excess supply or demand for dollars? Explain.

   b. Suppose that you bring a dollar to the Treasury and ask the Treasury to exchange it for yen. How many yen will the Treasury be obliged to give you for the dollar? Can you point to any problems that might arise as a result of the fixed exchange rate in the long run?

4. Describe the circumstances that led to the rise of the United States current account deficit during the 1980s.

5. Why is borrowing to finance a current account deficit so dangerous for a developing country? Explain the nature of the long-run adjustment that will correct a current account deficit? Is this adjustment process painless for the developing country? Explain.

Answers to Questions

True-False Questions

1. False because it is a market for the exchange of currencies.
2. True
3. True
4. False because a currency depreciates if it requires more of that currency to buy another.
5. True
6. False because a weak currency helps exporters.
7. True
8. True
9. True
10. False because the balance of payments account shows a country's financial relationship with the rest of the world.
11. True
12. True
13. True
14. False because the capital account shows changes in asset holdings at home and abroad for a country.
15. True
16. False because imports of capital goods can lead to greater potential to export in the future.
17. True
18. True
19. False because low productivity tends to make domestic producers' goods more expensive.
20. True
21. True

Multiple Choice Questions

1. b	6. c	11. c	16. a
2. c	7. a	12. d	17. d
3. b	8. d	13. d	18. a
4. a	9. c	14. c	19. b
5. c	10. a	15. c	20. b

Problem

1. a. These exchange rates are not mutually consistent. If they were, then the yen/mark exchange rate would be 26.67. The yen is overvalued at the 20 yen/mark exchange rate.

   b. It is possible. 1000 yen will buy 50 marks which can be traded for $16.67 that will purchase 1333.3 yen.

   c. The rates will come into alignment because people will continue to buy marks with yen and dollars with marks thus increasing the value of the mark and the dollar and decreasing the value of the yen.

Discussion Questions

1. a. If the price of a dollar in pesos is low, then people will want to trade pesos for more dollars than if the price of a dollar in pesos is high.

   b. As the peso price of a dollar increases, holders of dollars will want to supply more of them for pesos.

CHAPTER 17   EXCHANGE RATES   THE WORLD ECONOMY   169

2. A sketch of the supply and demand diagram is shown here.

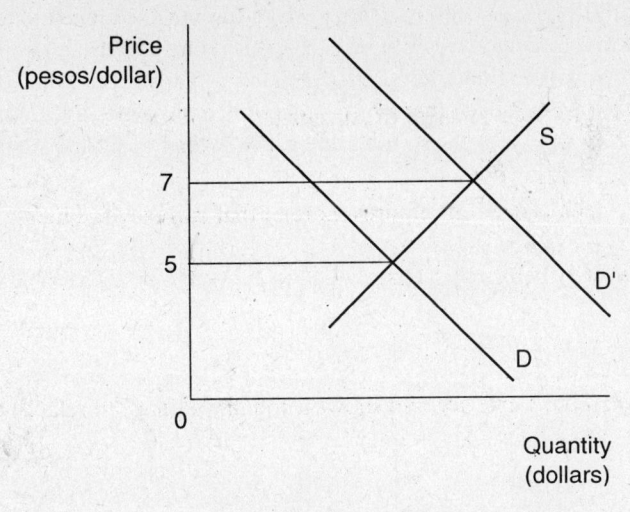

[Graph: Price (pesos/dollar) vs Quantity (dollars), showing supply curve S, demand curves D and D', with equilibrium prices at 5 and 7]

The shift in the demand curve from D to D' represents a depreciation in the peso relative to the dollar. The dollar has strengthened. Whether this is good or bad depends on your situation. If you are a Mexican importer of American goods, then this is bad because American goods will cost more in pesos. However, if you are an American importing Mexican goods, then this is good because a dollar will purchase more pesos.

3. a. A sketch of the graph depicting this situation is shown here.

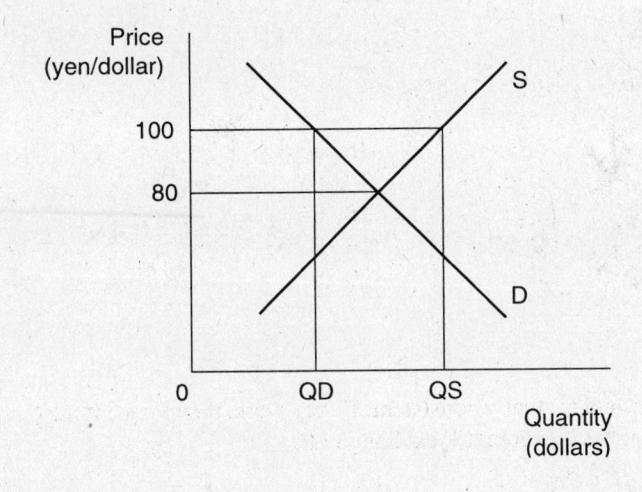

[Graph: Price (yen/dollar) vs Quantity (dollars), showing supply curve S, demand curve D, with prices 100 and 80, and quantities QD and QS marked]

At 100 yen per dollar there is an excess supply of dollars because the quantity supplied denoted with QS is greater than the quantity demanded denoted by QD.

b. For every dollar, the Treasury will have to give up 100 yen. The biggest problem for the Treasury might be how to maintain adequate amounts of yen. In a worst case scenario, the Treasury might have to borrow yen on the market in order to maintain the exchange rate at 100 yen per dollar.

4. A combination of circumstances contributed to the current account deficit during the 1980s. Factors include the strong dollar arising from relatively high interest rates in the United States. High interest rates were caused in part by the federal budget deficit. Also, the United States was perceived to be a good place to invest which contributed strength to the dollar. The inability of some American producers to compete in some foreign markets also contributed to the current account deficit.

5. Borrowing to finance a current account deficit becomes problematic when the debt service rises to levels that are difficult to sustain. Exports must be substantial to earn enough foreign exchange to pay the interest on the debt. A country won't be able to borrow forever if the debt service keeps rising because it simply won't be able to meet the interest obligations and no one will lend any longer. As a country imports more than it exports over a long period of time, its currency will weaken relative to others making imports more expensive. However, the country's exports look more attractive as the currency weakens so the trade gap will tend to shrink over time.

CHAPTER 18

ECONOMIC PROBLEMS OF LESS-DEVELOPED COUNTRIES

Chapter Summary

A friend of Ernest Hemingway, the celebrated American novelist, once said to him: "The rich are different from us," to which Hemingway replied: "Yes, they have more money." What Hemingway said was true, of course, but he really missed the point. What differentiates the rich from the poor is not their incomes, but the fact that the poor are not in a position not to be poor. Poverty is a result; the conditions of poverty are the cause. That's what this chapter is about. It examines the conditions that keep low-income, less-developed countries of Asia, Africa, and Latin America trapped in national poverty.

The per capita incomes of the less-developed countries (LDCs) vary substantially. It was, in 1988, only $120 in Ethiopia. Of course, some Ethiopians are considerably richer than you are, but for the population as a whole—per capita income means the total income of the country divided by its total population—poverty is a frightful reality. Per capita income in South Korea, on the other hand, was $3,600. With few exceptions (mostly Asian), per capita incomes in the LDCs grow very slowly, some not at all. One reason: High rates of population growth versus low rates of GDP growth.

The rich countries of the western world continue to make large investments in human capital that contribute significantly to their high and growing per capita incomes. LDCs, on the other hand, find it difficult, in some cases, impossible, to make these investments. The opportunity cost—what they must give up to make these investments—is extraordinarily high because many of the LDCs are living close to subsistence. The benefits from investments in human capital occur only in the long run—too long for many of these countries.

LDCs are characterized by economic dualism which refers to the co-existence within the country of two separate and distinct economic sectors. One is modern and connected to the rest of the world through trade and investments; the other is traditional—essentially in low-level agriculture or marginal service-related activity—which is as remote from the modern world as Mars. The vast majority of those in the traditional sector are trapped in their conditions for reasons that are as much cultural, psychological, and political as they are economic. Workers in the traditional sector earn low wages because of a low level of capital intensity, traditional technology, and weak prices while workers in the LDCs' modern sector earn higher wages, working with modern technology and producing higher priced goods for export.

Political instability plays an important role by creating uncertainty that undermines economic decision making. Traditional societies hold value systems that tend to reject the materialist and scientific approaches to development. Most important, the absence of an adequate infrastructure—transportation and communications systems, electric grids, money and banking institutions, schools, health and sanitation systems—inhibits development. Why should peasants increase output beyond local needs when there are no transportation and marketing facilities that allow them to sell the surplus?

What can they do? Many different development strategies are suggested for LDCs. One is the big-push. The idea behind the big-push strategy is this: Potential investments never get made because each depends on there being a market for their output. If the market's not there, why invest? The big-push overcomes this block by undertaking a massive set of interrelated investments, all at once, that create interrelated demands for and supplies of each other's goods. In other words, investments, production, and markets are created simultaneously. Who does it? Typically, the LDC's government orchestrates a big-push by coordinating infrastructure and development investments and their financing over the long run. One rationale for the government to plan and coordinate the big-push is that the government has a longer time horizon than do private entrepreneurs.

Another approach to LDC development is the unbalanced strategy. Rather than relying on government to direct development efforts, the unbalanced development strategy focuses on entrepreneurs doing most of the investment and financing of profitable projects. Government still plays a role by investing in infrastructure. With an infrastructure in place, private entrepreneurs pursue investments that create backward and forward linkages in the economy. New demands and supplies are created through new investment, existing markets expand and new markets are created in the process. This strategy is called unbalanced because with each new investment an imbalance is created between new supplies that create new demands in new markets. The new demands are called forward linkages. These demands are met because firms, now with a market for their goods, will supply them. These supplies are called backward linkages.

Foreign direct investment can also promote economic development. It gives LDCs capital without their having to sacrifice an already minimal standard of living. Foreign direct investment also gives LDCs access to markets in the industrial economies. Because of the LDCs' prior experience with foreign direct investment—colonialism—they have become very cautious, maybe too cautious, about allowing foreign direct investment.

Foreign economic aid is another source of funds for development. Governments in the developed world provide aid to governments in LDCs in the form of either loans or grants. In the United States, our foreign economic aid programs are administered by the Agency for International Development (AID) in the Department of State.

In too many cases, LDCs are more interested in importing military goods than capital goods. And, too, often, these war-related imports create considerable international debt for the LDCs which interferes with their economic development. Arms imports have been scaled down somewhat since 1987 due primarily to the end of the Cold War. The desire to maintain political stability for governments in LDC countries is a powerful incentive for high levels of arms purchases.

Key Terms — Test your comprehension by defining and explaining the significance of these terms.

less-developed countries
human capital
economic dualism
infrastructure
big-push
forward linkage
backward linkage

True-False Questions — If a statement is false, explain why.

1. In spite of their differences in national and per capita incomes, the development problems that LDCs and industrialized countries face are basically the same. (T/F)

2. Prior to the 1950s, LDCs were prejudicially described as economically backward and underdeveloped. (T/F)

3. Per capita income levels among many of the LDCs are at or near subsistence. (T/F)

4. In spite of low level of income, growth rates of per capita income in LDCs average well above the five percent per year mark. (T/F)

5. LDCs are characterized by relatively high birth rates and falling death rates. (T/F)

6. Growth rates for industrial output lag behind growth rates for agricultural output in LDC countries. (T/F)

CHAPTER 18   ECONOMIC PROBLEMS OF LESS-DEVELOPED COUNTRIES

7. LDCs would be able to make larger investments in human capital if production levels were above subsistence. (T/F)

8. Infant mortality is inversely related to both the number of people per physician and the income level. (T/F)

9. Economic dualism refers to the adoption of both Keynesian and monetarist policies for economic development. (T/F)

10. Wage rates in the traditional sector tend to be higher than those in the modern sector where workers are exploited by multinational corporations. (T/F)

11. Political instability in LDC countries can lead to uncertainty about the nature of property rights. (T/F)

12. Traditional methods of production in LDC countries emphasize the production of surpluses for sale in the world market. (T/F)

13. A country's infrastructure consists of its basic institutions and the public facilities like transportation and communication systems upon which development depends. (T/F)

14. A big-push development strategy relies on coordinated increases in investment in several industries at once in order to create interlocking markets for output. (T/F)

15. The big-push development strategy can be supported through government spending that is supported by tax revenues and by foreign investment. (T/F)

16. Forward linkages consist of new opportunities for profitable investment in industries that use the output from existing industries as inputs. (T/F)

17. Increases in the demand for steel and plastics that come as a result of growth in the automobile industry are examples of backward linkages. (T/F)

18. Unbalanced development strategies rely more on investments by entrepreneurs than on government spending initiatives. (T/F)

19. Foreign direct investment can shift an LDC's production possibilities curve to the right. (T/F)

20. Arms imports by LDC countries have risen sharply since 1987. (T/F)

Multiple Choice Questions

1. LDCs are poor because
   a. they choose to be.
   b. of colonial exploitation.
   c. of exploitation by multinationals.
   d. the world they inhabit affords them little choice.
   e. of communist dictators.

2. Levels of income have jumped dramatically in recent years in all of the following countries except
   a. Brazil.
   b. South Korea.
   c. Hong Kong.
   d. Ethiopia.
   e. Taiwan.

3. One of the fastest growing LDC countries in recent years has been
   a. Zaire.
   b. Zambia.
   c. South Korea.
   d. Jamaica.
   e. Bolivia.

4. The primary reasons for rapid population growth in LDCs are
   a. declining birth and death rates.
   b. declining birth rates and rising death rates.
   c. rising birth rates and falling death rates.
   d. death rates that are falling faster than birth rates.
   e. the complete lack of family planning.

5. The most important source of economic growth in LDCs is from
   a. the agricultural sector.
   b. the industrial sector.
   c. foreign trade.
   d. government spending.
   e. population growth.

6. It is possible to add significantly to a country's stock of human capital by
   a. investing in physical capital.
   b. lowering interest rates.
   c. improving the infrastructure.
   d. insuring that children receive primary education.
   e. cutting government regulations.

7. Economic dualism is best represented by a country where
   a. some 20 percent of the population works for high wages in the modern sector and the rest work in the traditional sector.
   b. the population is 80 percent urban and 20 percent rural.
   c. production is virtually all agricultural compared to the industrialized countries nearby.
   d. production goes on with high tech and low tech methods in industry.
   e. many people have jobs in both agriculture and industry.

8. Economic development can proceed more easily in a country where property rights are
   a. more secure.
   b. in the hands of the people.
   c. most valuable.
   d. uncertain.
   e. reassigned by a revolution.

9. If a peasant in an LDC sticks to traditional methods of agriculture instead of adopting modern technology, it is likely that
   a. production will be much more secure.
   b. growth rates in output will be slower.
   c. growth rates in output will be more rapid.
   d. investment in agriculture will be high.
   e. foreign multinationals will invest more.

10. Much of the investment in infrastructure is likely to be funded by the government in an LDC because the infrastructure consists largely of
    a. public goods.
    b. private goods.
    c. risky assets.
    d. capital goods.
    e. consumer goods.

11. A country experiencing the poverty trap will find economic development to be difficult because
    a. foreign aid is nonexistent.
    b. production is so close to subsistence that investment is made impossible.
    c. there is a lack of potential entrepreneurs in the country.
    d. the country is probably badly governed.
    e. environmental damage is so severe that economic development is no longer possible.

12. A big-push development strategy emphasizes investment in
    a. one key industry.
    b. the production of consumer goods for immediate marketing.
    c. several industries at once that have interlocking markets.
    d. the oil industry.
    e. industries that require the most investment (big-push) to get going.

13. Government investment is emphasized by advocates of the big-push strategy because
    a. only government has the resources to finance the large investments required.
    b. private investment is already tapped completely.
    c. the government is likely to have a longer time horizon than private investors.
    d. private investors are incompetent.
    e. only the government has the personnel to implement and manage the big-push in highly technical industries.

14. The unbalanced development strategy is unbalanced because
    a. governments that undertake this approach are unstable.
    b. forward linkages are stronger than backward linkages.
    c. backward linkages are stronger than forward linkages.
    d. an imbalance results between supply capacity and the creation of new demands.
    e. government's role is completely eliminated so the process is completely private.

15. Backward linkages in the unbalanced development strategy relate to increases in
    a. demands for the products of already-existing industries.
    b. demands for the products of the backward sector.
    c. traditional practices that emerge in opposition to modernization.
    d. links between businesses in the traditional sector.
    e. links with government agencies that used to sponsor fledgling private sector businesses.

16. Foreign direct investment has the advantage that _____, which has to be weighed against the disadvantage that _____.
    a. growth is much faster; the environment is destroyed
    b. investment is financed by foreigners; profits may be sent abroad
    c. investment in foreign countries is profitable; investment at home languishes
    d. domestic firms get funding; foreign firms lose employment
    e. multinationals profit enormously; industrialized nations suffer

17. United States foreign economic aid programs since World War II have consisted mostly of
    a. arms exports.
    b. direct food relief.
    c. grants for development.
    d. low interest loans.
    e. high interest short-term loans.

18. Even though military expenditures by LDC countries rose by 1.7 percent per year between 1980 and 1991, arms imports began to
    a. rise at an even faster rate.
    b. fall in all regions except the Middle East after 1987.
    c. fall in all regions except for Asia after 1987.
    d. fall in all regions except the former Soviet republics after 1991.
    e. fall in all regions of the world after 1987.

19. The main reason for the existence of forward linkages in the unbalanced development strategy is that investments in one industry will result in
    a. lower interest rates for other investors in other industries.
    b. savings that can be transmitted to other industries.
    c. opportunities for investment in new industries that use the output of the first as inputs.
    d. higher prices for retailers in urban regions where the investment is occurring.
    e. the expansion of infrastructure investment in the traditional sector.

20. All of the following are reasons for the low level of development in the traditional sector of an LDC except
    a. low levels of literacy.
    b. low levels of capital per person.
    c. poor infrastructure.
    d. attitudes opposed to modernization.
    e. exploitation over centuries by multinationals.

Discussion Questions

1. How does the rapid growth in agricultural output in industrialized countries like the United States contribute to problems for developing countries?

2. Contrast the role of government in the big-push development strategy and the unbalanced strategy.

3. Using your knowledge of forward and backward linkages, describe the expansion of the railroad in U.S. economic development.

4. What is the opportunity cost of spending on arms imports for a developing country?

5. Could extreme forms of economic dualism create political tensions in a less-developed country? Explain why.

Answers to Questions

True-False Questions

1. False because the economic problems facing LDCs have to do with such basic issues as producing subsistence levels of output.
2. True
3. True
4. False because most LDCs are experiencing slow growth or economic stagnation.
5. True
6. False because the industrial sector was the source of most growth.
7. True
8. True
9. False because economic dualism refers to the existence of a modern sector typified by high wage rates and a traditional sector where wage rates are stuck at subsistence.
10. False because wage rates are higher in the modern sector.
11. True
12. False because methods of production in the traditional sector of LDCs are usually geared toward subsistence production.
13. True
14. True
15. True
16. True
17. True
18. True
19. True
20. False because they have fallen off somewhat since the end of the Cold War.

Multiple Choice Questions

1. d	6. d	11. b	16. b
2. d	7. a	12. c	17. c
3. c	8. a	13. c	18. e
4. d	9. b	14. d	19. c
5. b	10. a	15. a	20. e

Discussion Questions

1. Rapid growth in agricultural output in the United States and other industrial countries lowers the world price of agricultural goods, making it more difficult for LDCs to improve their standard of living through exports.

2. The government plays a much larger role in the big-push approach than in the unbalanced approach. The government's role is paramount in the big-push approach because many industries with interlocking markets are involved in the process all at once and the effort needs to be coordinated. Government is in a better position to coordinate. Also, government has a longer time horizon than private investors. However, government does play an important role in infrastructure development in both approaches. Also, government may encourage investment in select industries in the unbalanced approach.

3. The railroad opened up new markets for manufactured goods in the west. These are forward linkages. Also, the railroad required large inputs of iron, steel, coal, lumber and other products in addition to labor. These are backward linkages.

4. Suppose that arms expenditures of LDCs are eliminated and the funds are devoted to investment in productive capital. Rates of economic growth would accelerate and living standards would improve. This represents a significant opportunity cost. However, the expenditures on arms imports may be understandable if the LDC's national security is threatened in a significant way.

5. Extreme forms of economic dualism could create political tensions in a less-developed country. Economic dualism contributes to gross inequality in the income distribution. The traditional sector is left observing improving conditions in the modern sector while the conditions in the traditional sector remain unchanged. Inequality breeds tension in this sort of situation.

CHAPTER 19

THEORIES OF COMPARATIVE ECONOMIC SYSTEMS

Chapter Summary

Marx's theory of economic systems is deterministic. Society evolves from one economic system to the next in a sequence determined by the state of technology. One system creates the conditions for the next. Marx envisioned societies progressing from primitive communism to feudalism to capitalism to socialism and, finally, to communism. The process that Marx used to explain the transition from one system to the next is the dialectics. There are three parts to the dialectics: First, a thesis—the existing set of institutions, structures, activities and relations—which contains a inherent contradiction or antithesis. Second, the antithesis, representing the source of conflict in the thesis. Marx identified property as a source of conflict. The conflict involves those who own property and those who don't. Over time, the contradictions or conflict within the thesis increases to the point where the thesis can no longer contain the conflict. An explosion occurs, shattering the thesis out of which emerges the synthesis. Third, the synthesis, which is a new thesis containing some of the elements of the old and some new.

Marx's dialectics can be used to explain the transformation from feudalism to capitalism. Feudalism, based in land property and land technology, is characterized by two major classes: land owners and peasants. One exploits, the other works. Out of the peasant class emerges a class of merchants and manufacturers—embryonic at first—whose interests are in conflict with those of the dominant feudal classes. Eventually, manufacturing technology comes to dominate the system, forcing it to change—via revolution, most likely—from feudalism to capitalism. The new property form is capital, and the two major classes are capitalists and workers. One exploits, the other works. Capitalism, too, contains contradictions and the seeds of its own destruction. Factory-based technology brings workers together and imposes both increasing misery and class solidarity on them. More and more workers end up facing fewer and fewer capitalists as monopoly power in capitalism increases. Finally, the workers seize control of the enormous productive power that capitalism has created so that private property is socialized. Socialism is a temporary stage on the way to communism. Under communism, production is organized according to a plan where people contribute to production according to ability and receive according to need. There is no need for a state to guard the interests of the propertied class since resources are held communally. The state simply withers away under communism.

Marx's stage theory is deterministic in the sense that it doesn't allow countries to choose their economic systems. Most economists don't buy into Marx's theory. They argue that societies do have some degree of choice. Society is free to choose its political and economic systems. Democracies tend to have market economies. This is no accident because democracies and market economies both emphasize freedom of expression and activity. A variety of economic systems exists from which societies can choose. This chapter examines these choices.

Capitalism and market socialism are two types of economic systems that provide individuals with the right to express economic choice. Capitalism is based on private property. Within established rules, individuals are allowed to use their property as they see fit. Buyers and sellers exchange property in markets. Property may generate income that its owners have a right to claim under capitalism. While inequities may arise between owners of property and those who don't, the incomes people earn under capitalism are supposed to be linked to effort. Income is a reward for effort.

Market socialism presents a contrast to capitalism with the state owning all property except labor. However, individuals choose what they want to buy in the market and these choices signal to the state what is to be produced. One difference between socialist markets and capitalist markets is that the state sets price initially in the socialist market. If a price is too low, an excess demand for goods arises and this signals the state to raise the price. Equilibrium prices are reached via a process of trial and error. Advocates of market socialism argue that the system preserves the efficiency advantages of capitalism while eliminating the unearned incomes associated with property ownership that give rise to income inequality. Moreover, the investment decision is left in the hands of the state rather than consumers, thus contributing to a better growth performance for a market socialist economy over time. Capitalism emphasizes liberty while market socialism emphasizes equality.

Market socialism remains a theoretical construct. The type of socialism that has existed is state socialism. Under state socialism, such as existed in the former Soviet Union, the state not only controls ownership of resources, but it determines what is to be produced and the plan according to which production will occur. An economic plan can be constructed by organizing data on the inputs needed to produce the variety of commodities in the economy. One way to organize the data on inputs and outputs is in the form of a matrix called an input-output table. Once a consistent plan is developed where there are sufficient inputs to produce each of the planned outputs, the state can construct a set of prices. These prices may or may not bear any relationship to the demand and supply conditions in particular markets. A state bank issues sufficient money to finance the transactions called for in the plan. The plan is put into action and problems with plan fulfillment are addressed by giving certain industries the highest priority as resources are allocated between competing uses. Frequently, the interests of consumers are pushed to the side as heavy industry is given the greatest emphasis.

Fascism had its heyday in the 1930s in Germany, Italy, and Spain. Property is privately owned under fascism, but economic sovereignty is vested in the state. The state organizes business, labor and the government into a cooperative unit designed to achieve state goals. Fascist economic systems are linked to authoritarian political regimes. Fascists justify their choice on the basis that it promotes high rates of economic growth. Given the character of the political regime in power in fascist states and the emphasis on economic growth, fascism is similar to state socialism.

The pure forms of economic systems outlined here do not exist in the real world. The economic systems that societies have chosen form a spectrum from closer to pure capitalism—like the United States through countries that have some socialist characteristics such as France, Germany, and Sweden—to state socialist economies like China and North Korea. Many economies including those in eastern Europe and the region that encompassed the Soviet Union are now in transition from state socialism to market-based systems. This process emphasizes the extent to which a society can manipulate its economic system.

Key Terms — Test your comprehension by defining and explaining the significance of these terms.

nomadic economic system
feudalism
capitalism
socialism
communism
dialectics
thesis
antithesis

synthesis
historical materialism
market socialism
state socialism
input-output table
economic plan
fascism
privatization

True-False Questions — If a statement is false, explain why.

1. According to Karl Marx, it is impossible for a society to choose its economic system. (T/F)

2. Marx's theory of economic systems is described as deterministic because it is based on states of technology. (T/F)

3. The thesis in Marx's dialectics is the collection of all the key elements that make up a functional society. (T/F)

4. A basic conflict in capitalist society, according to Marx, is between the young and the old. (T/F)

5. Under feudalism, harmony existed among merchants, manufacturers, and the owners of feudal estates. (T/F)

6. Marx predicted that capitalist production would become concentrated in the hands of the few. (T/F)

7. Socialism is the end-stage of economic evolution in Marxist theory. (T/F)

8. In a nondeterministic theory of economic systems, historical materialism is used to describe the choices that a society has among various types of economic systems. (T/F)

9. Capitalism allows owners of property to claim the income that the property can generate. (T/F)

10. In market socialism, the state determines where workers will be employed. (T/F)

11. In market socialism, prices are driven to equilibrium by trial and error. (T/F)

12. The investment decision is left to workers in market socialism. (T/F)

13. Capitalism emphasizes liberty; market socialism emphasizes equality. (T/F)

14. In its pure form, state socialism is a completely planned economic system. (T/F)

15. An input-output table shows the number of units of various inputs that are required to produce specific quantities of different outputs. (T/F)

16. Planned economies have the advantage that all aspects of the plan are fulfilled virtually every year. (T/F)

17. Prices are allowed to be set by market demand and market supply under state socialism. (T/F)

18. Production under state socialism is based on planners' preferences rather than consumer's preferences. (T/F)

19. Resources are state-owned under fascism. (T/F)

20. The United States comes as close to pure capitalism as any other country in the world today. (T/F)

21. French indicative planning is much like planning that was used in the former Soviet Union. (T/F)

22. Gosplan was the name of the Soviet planning agency and Gosbank was the name of the state bank. (T/F)

Multiple Choice Questions

1. A theory that maintains it is impossible for a society to choose its economic system is
   a. capitalist.
   b. socialist.
   c. fascist.
   d. deterministic.
   e. nondeterministic.

2. Marx's dialectics refer to the key elements of a functional society as the
   a. thesis.
   b. antithesis.
   c. property right.
   d. synthesis.
   e. feudal stage.

3. The dominant property form in feudalism is
   a. labor.
   b. land.
   c. capital.
   d. agriculture.
   e. manufacturing.

4. All of the following are examples of merchants' and manufacturers' behavior under feudalism that contributed to the rise of capitalism except
   a. advancing production technology.
   b. investment in transportation systems such as roads.
   c. pushing for freer trade.
   d. attracting peasant labor from the countryside to the city.
   e. forming alliances with the feudal estate owners to preserve their manors for the future.

5. The impact of capitalist technology on workers in the factories was, according to Marx,
   a. to give them an appreciation for modern machinery.
   b. to lessen class tensions.
   c. to create class solidarity.
   d. to create full employment by increasing workers' productivity.
   e. to improve their standard of living.

6. Under communism, the state withers away because
   a. production is planned.
   b. production has ceased.
   c. capitalists are enlightened.
   d. classes no longer exist.
   e. property is transferred to the state.

7. Income that is generated under capitalism, but not under market socialism, is
   a. wages.
   b. salaries.
   c. profit.
   d. fringe benefits.
   e. transfer payments.

8. One argument that might be used to justify the income inequality inherent in a capitalist system is that
   a. the rich donate heavily to aid programs for the poor.
   b. income differences reflect the linkage between effort and reward.
   c. all poor people are inherently unproductive.
   d. inequality in the income distribution is impossible to eliminate.
   e. everyone has an equal chance at becoming rich.

9. The likely response to excess demand in a market in a market socialist economy is for
   a. the price to rise toward the equilibrium.
   b. the price to fall toward the equilibrium.
   c. the state to increase the price.
   d. the state to decrease the price.
   e. ration coupons to be issued.

10. One advantage of market socialism, according to its proponents, is that
    a. income inequality is completely eliminated.
    b. investment decision making is placed in the hands of the state.
    c. markets are more competitive.
    d. bankruptcy is impossible.
    e. managers have no decision-making role in the day-to-day operations of the firm.

11. The difference between market socialism and state socialism is that under state socialism
    a. the market is used more extensively as a guide to resource allocation.
    b. the economic plan completely replaces the market.
    c. firms, although owned by the state, are still very competitive.
    d. equilibrium prices are lower.
    e. consumer sovereignty dictates what will be produced by the state.

12. The columns in an input-output table of an economic plan show
    a. for every industry, the quantities of inputs required to produce a quantity of output.
    b. the allocation of the industries' outputs to other sectors.
    c. the production possibilities of every industry.
    d. how income equality is achieved among industries.
    e. how firms are able to maximize output in each industry.

13. The highest priority target of an economic plan under state socialism is
    a. consumer goods production.
    b. agriculture.
    c. heavy industry.
    d. light industry.
    e. services.

14. A fascist state, according to its proponents, organizes business, labor, and government into a cooperative unit to
    a. achieve maximum profits for businesses.
    b. eliminate unemployment.
    c. minimize class tensions.
    d. achieve high rates of economic growth.
    e. complete the socialist revolution.

15. The main difference between state socialism and fascism is that property ownership under state socialism is _____ and under fascism it is _____.
    a. state; public
    b. public; state
    c. communal; private
    d. state; private
    e. state; cooperative

16. French indicative planning was designed to be
    a. the first-stage outline of an economic plan.
    b. a set of guidelines for private industry.
    c. a set of compulsory consumption targets.
    d. a set of compulsory industrial targets.
    e. a complete replacement for the market.

17. Farms in the former Soviet Union were
    a. privately held by peasants.
    b. managed communally by the villages.
    c. either state farms or collective farms.
    d. managed like factory operations.
    e. completely state owned.

Discussion Questions

1. Why would Marx have viewed a socialist economic system in Ethiopia today as absurd?

2. Briefly explain Marx's view that feudalism and capitalism contain the seeds of their own destruction.

3. How is a society's choice of a political system related to its choice of an economic system?

4. Contrast the functioning of markets in a capitalist system and a market socialist system.

5. Explain how an input-output table can be used to organize planning in a state socialist economy. Are there problems associated with this approach to resource allocation? Discuss.

Answers to Questions

True-False Questions

1. True
2. True
3. True
4. False because the basic conflict is between those who own property and those who don't.
5. False because the interests of merchants and manufacturers were opposed to those of landlords.
6. True
7. False because communism is the end stage.
8. False because historical materialism is a Marxist or deterministic idea.
9. True
10. False because workers choose their occupations under market socialism.
11. True
12. False because investment is determined by the state under market socialism.
13. True
14. True
15. True
16. False because plan fulfillment is difficult to achieve for planned economies.
17. False because the state makes up a system of prices according to its preferences.
18. True
19. False because property is privately owned.
20. True
21. False because indicative planning only sets guidelines for French industry.
22. True

Multiple Choice Questions

1. d	6. d	11. b	16. b
2. a	7. c	12. a	17. c
3. b	8. b	13. c	
4. e	9. c	14. d	
5. c	10. b	15. d	

Discussion Questions

1. Marx would have viewed socialism in Ethiopia as absurd because Ethiopia was not sufficiently advanced technologically to be a socialist economy. It is still a nomadic agricultural society today.

2. Feudalism was based on landed property worked by exploited peasants. Emerging capitalism required labor. Opportunities in capitalist industries drew peasants away from the estates. Also, the feudal landowners' tastes for manufactured goods and imports contributed to the growth of the capitalist class. Capitalists gained power in society as their capitalist technology dominated. Free trade was one result that hastened the demise of feudalism.

    Under capitalism, changing technologies created the conditions for class conflict. Capitalists who adopt new technologies competed against those who didn't, driving them into bankruptcy and into the ranks of workers. Industries became concentrated in the hands of the few. Increasing misery and increasing numbers created class solidarity among workers that eventually led them to seize power from the capitalists. Private ownership was abolished, and socialism emerged.

3. Democracies, allowing freedom to vote, tend to be associated with market societies where freedom to exercise all forms of productive activity is promoted. In authoritarian societies, the economic system tends toward state socialism or fascism, each with limited freedom of expression for individuals and significant central direction from the state.

4. You know how markets function in a capitalist system (or at least you should by this chapter!). In a market socialist system, consumers buy and firms produce in response to consumer tastes just like they do in capitalism. However, the price is set initially by the state and is changed over time—trial and error—in response to excess demands or excess supplies in particular markets. In this way, equilibrium prices are eventually achieved.

5. An input-output table shows how outputs of one industry are the inputs in other industries. A basic problem is getting accurate data to construct the table. Unanticipated problems in particular industries—lack of resources, for example—lead to bottlenecks that magnify across all industries. Fulfilling planned production targets becomes impossible. In these cases, priorities are given. Some targets are sacrificed for others; typically, consumer goods are sacrificed for heavy industry.